Peru

Bolivia

Ecuador

The Indian Andes

PERU, BOLIVIA, ECUADOR

The Indian Andes

Charles Paul May

Thomas Nelson Inc.

The "rich hill" in Potosí, Bolivia

All photographs are by Charles Paul May with the exception of the following: pp. 136, 158, Fritz Albert, University of Wisconsin; pp. 125, 128, Richard Harrington; pp. 183, 184, Museum of Art, Lima, Peru; p. 47, Pan American Airways; pp. 10, 15, 16, 25, 34, 35, 44, 46, 58, 63, 82, 89, 94, 96, 100, 109, 122 (insert), 126, 127, 129, 148, 151, 167, 169, 172, 199, 203, 208, 210, Pan American Union; p. 205, Peace Corps; p. 97, Esther Glaser Parada, Peace Corps; pp. 103, 150, 156, 160, 165, 166, 188, Paul Conklin, Peace Corps; p. 187, Wylie L. Williams, Jr. Permission is gratefully acknowledged.

To

Sally, Olin, Marcia, Cathie, Sharon, and Jane Emens

and

to Jack Bostick

Library of Congress Catalog Card Number: 74-82915

Printed in the United States of America

Acknowledgments

1706968

The author wishes to express his thanks to Alfredo Abad, Andrés Achata Cabrera, Mary Luz Barreda, Father Judson Bishop, Thomas W. Brown, Mr. and Mrs. Gerald Cashman, Richard Chiriboga, Jorge Davila, Sister Patricia Downs, Elsa Echalar, Elvira Gálvez, Dr. Giddings, Dr. and Mrs. Gordon Gilkes, Rodolfo Holzmann, Howard W. Huskey, Peter Jensen, Sara Joffré, Franz Juliusberger, Sister Ruth Payne, Mr. and Mrs. Paul Price, Jackelyne Portal Purdy, Patricia Reagan, Elizabeth Reyes, Gladys Rivas, Luz Robles, Cora L. Russ, Enrique Salcedo, Gustavo Salcedo, Marjorie Smith, Roy Smith, Francisco Stastny, and Wylie L. Williams, Jr.

Peru

Bolivia

Ecuador

COLOMBIA

QUATOR · Otavalo

QUITO ★

ECUADOR

Mt. Chimborazo ▲

Riobamba

Salinas

Guayaquil

Gulf of Cuenca
Guayaquil

Zamora

Napo River

Amazon River

Iquitos

PERU

Cajamarca

Chimbote

▲ Mt. Huascarán

LA MONTAÑA

A
N
D
E
S

PACIFIC OCEAN

Callao ★ LIMA

M
O
U
N
T
A
I
N
S

Machu Picchu

Cuzco

BRAZIL

El Misti

Arequipa ▲

Lake Titicaca

BOLIVIA

ALTIPLANO

★ LA PAZ

· Cochabamba

· Santa Cruz

Oruro

★ SUCRE

Potosí

GALAPAGOS ISLANDS

7

Contents

The clock tower, once a beacon light, is a famous landmark along the Guayas River waterfront at Guayaquil

Not Quite Paradise

In each of the Andes republics you can find a spot that some traveler has compared to the Garden of Eden. Thirty-five miles north of Cuzco, Peru offers a typical example—the Yucay Valley. It rates such elegant titles as "vale of imperial delights" or, if you prefer simpler descriptions, "a bit of Paradise." Bolivia's wide valley around Cochabamba ranks as that country's major resort area today, while the earliest Spanish explorers in what is now Ecuador saw the present site of Quito as a place of rare beauty. Many other so-called Edens can be found in each of these three countries.

The descendants of Quechua, Aymara, and Quitu Indians, who battle the rocky soils of these valleys to make a poor living, have trouble comparing their home territories to the Paradise of which missionaries eagerly tell them. Did Adam and Eve stub bare toes on clods and stones the way shoeless teen-age girls and boys do as they turn the land with spades or ox-drawn plows? If the residents of Paradise could go without clothes until driven from their happy homeland, they obviously lived in a place far removed from the high Andes. In these valleys women wear two or more skirts and as many petticoats to keep warm, perhaps chewing a narcotic as well to provide some "inner fire."

Near the coasts of Peru and Ecuador and along the Amazon River, away from chill mountains, other native peoples also find life less than ideal or idyllic. While hacking paths through jungle or using pointed sticks to pierce sun-hardened or root-strewn land, they swat at blood-hungry insects and watch for twelve-foot snakes. Sweat bathes

An Andean mother weaves cloth outside her family's home which is made of stone and thatch, common building materials in the high mountains of Bolivia

11

Older jungle Indians dress in clothing of grass as their ancestors did. These Yaguas leave their huts along a tributary of the Amazon to go to their farms

their backs and legs. Though some go without clothes, hunting and food gathering keep them from enjoying a life comparable to that in Eden. Besides, the white man leaves few areas they can call entirely their own or that they can inhabit in the age-old ways of their ancestors. Intruders, whether armed with spears, guns, Bibles, hoes, or axes, mean change, often rapid change. And rapid alterations frequently spell death for people attuned to the slow changes of the ages. Paradises? Hardly. Only because we compare them with even more rugged areas nearby do they vaguely resemble gardens of Eden.

Peru, Bolivia, and Ecuador are truly lands of the Andes, and all three countries have large Indian populations. Inevitably they face many of the same problems, which are often the same ones man has faced since coming to the area. Though volcanoes and earthquakes occasionally vary some of their shapes, the mountains present basically

12

the same obstacles they did when humans first came to them. Along with being chilly much of the time, they offer a short growing season except in some of the low valleys. A short season limits the crops people can cultivate successfully. Wind currents and temperatures above certain slopes cause most of the precipitation to fall repeatedly in the same areas, to the east, leaving others with practically no moisture. Partly as a result, Peru's coastal strip is mainly desert, though Ecuador has jungles reaching to the Pacific Ocean. With little or no rain, irrigation becomes necessary, but even some mountain-fed rivers peter away to mere rivulets during the summer dry season between December and March, until irrigation becomes impossible.

Plans made one day may be frustrated the next because of circumstances entirely beyond the control of human beings. Climates alter. Ecuador receives less and less rainfall every year. Salinas, on the Pacific Ocean west of Guayaquil, used to have enough rain so that a large reservoir was built nearby. This stored sufficient water to take care of the small city's needs. But it has been about a decade since the area experienced a good rainfall, so tank trucks now journey the eighty miles from Guayaquil to provide Salinas with water.

El Misti, the most famous volcanic peak of southern Peru, is surrounded by near-desert conditions

A few large rivers and a number of their tributaries serve as highways, but much of the time both rivers and mountains are barriers to travel. They also limit the amount of land suitable for agriculture. Some valley walls rise too abruptly for terracing, many peaks are too high to permit plant growth, and numerous streams in low regions create land too swampy for cultivation. Even where problems could be overcome, the local residents may make no move to tackle them. The people have had to surrender many individual and tribal rights to a central, national government. Let that government attend to the problems. That's what the politicians claim they will do every time there's an election. Not that the people expect much of them any more. There have been many elections and revolutions but few changes in the past. Tomorrow will undoubtedly be much the same as today.

The lack of governmental action brings up one of the great problems throughout Latin America and especially in Peru, Bolivia, and Ecuador. The politicians have little in common with the native peoples. Many of the men in government descend from European immigrants and openly or secretly consider themselves above mestizos and Indians. Even men of part-Indian blood look down on the men with little or no European heritage, and wherever such prejudices exist, progress for the lower classes will be slow.

Because mountains and rivers have stood between the various local peoples for thousands of years, men of one group have usually distrusted those of another. In addition to the natural barriers that separate various tribes, cultural differences have increased misunderstanding, for example, in the vicinity of Santa Cruz, Bolivia. The native people of the Santa Cruz region are descendants of the old jungle Indians rather than of the mountain groups. The early Spaniards called them *Cambas,* which means "no clothes." Besides lacking garments, they also lacked laws, a central government, and a strong religion; obviously, they were opposites of the well-organized Incas. As much as possible they went their separate ways, banding together only when war required. Reportedly, they were without strong personalities of their own, readily adapting to the ways of foreigners who came to live around them, and some observers say this remains true to the present time.

14

The Bolivian terrain presents a challenge for workmen, here attempting to lay oil pipelines through jungle and swampland

Today, when natives of the altiplano—the high plateau—go to Santa Cruz, they usually become more successful than the Cambas. They have had to work hard on the altiplano to stay alive, and when they go to other regions they continue to put forth the same amount of effort. The Cambas have never found it necessary to struggle as much as the Quechuas and see no reason to change. They give the people from the altiplano a cool welcome, saying, in effect, "Quechuas, go home." In Santa Cruz a statue of Christ stands with arms outstretched. The Cambas say he is a traffic cop telling the people from the altiplano to halt and go back.

If prejudices exist among the descendants of the old groups, what hope can there be for understanding between Indians and people of European descent? And without understanding, it seems likely that affairs in Ecuador, Peru, and Bolivia will continue much as they are today. Fortunately, this has at least a few positive aspects. Though they do fall short of Paradise, these colorful lands abound with varied peoples and a fascinating assortment of new and ancient customs, as well as exotic animals and beautiful scenery.

Ancient Peoples

Taken as one land area, Ecuador, Bolivia, and Peru divide roughly into three major regions—the coast, the mountains, and the eastern lowlands. Although Ecuador and Peru both have coasts along the Pacific Ocean, Bolivia, having lost its western section in a war with Chile, no longer has a coastal region.

The Land Takes Shape

At one time, perhaps a hundred million years ago, most of the region lay low and level. But beneath the land's surface the rocks lacked stability. Hot streams of molten materials sought ways to escape, while some rocks split or slid over one another. The resulting earthquakes and volcanoes must have, at times, heaved stones about like giant kernels of popcorn on a sizzling griddle. During the time this activity continued, which was off and on for perhaps seventy-five million years, the Andes Mountains built up until some of their peaks jostled clouds four miles above sea level. Volcanic eruptions and earthquakes still strike the sierra, as the mountain country is called, but they have ceased to pile rocks higher and higher.

The Andes should not be thought of as a ridge, like a picket fence, down the length of western South America. They include a series of parallel ridges, sometimes splitting wide apart, sometimes coming close together. There are valleys between the ridges and valleys within the ridges. In Bolivia the Andes reach their widest spread, about four hundred miles across. Between the high peaks stretch lofty plateaus, or

Peruvian natives wear ponchos of alpaca wool, felt monteras *(fancy hats), and* hojotas *(shoes) of thin leather in the mountains near Cuzco*

17

Farm buildings dot the altiplanos in Bolivia

altiplanos, which explains why these lands are sometimes called Republics of the Altiplano. Because the mountains stretch north of Ecuador, Peru, and Bolivia into Colombia and south into Chile and Argentina, these lands are also called the Lands of the Central Andes.

The formation of the Andes separated the west coast lowlands from those to the east. At the same time, by raising some of the ground into a chilly cloudland, the mountains counteracted the hot, humid atmosphere of the equator, making parts of northwestern South America more endurable than they would otherwise be. Yet nomadic peoples, fleeing enemies, seeking new land, or pursuing animals they hunted, moved into the uncomfortable low areas as well as the high ones. No land was too low or hot, even along the equator as it cuts across northern Ecuador; and few were too high or cold, even those in southern Bolivia that reach nearly to the temperate zone.

People Come from Somewhere

Because so much has been written about the Incas, we sometimes forget that other Indians preceded them in the lands now known as Bolivia, Ecuador, and Peru. We also overlook groups living at the

18

same time as the Incas. No one knows for sure who the first groups were or how they reached northwestern South America. Most men who study past cultures agree that some Orientals came to the New World by way of northeast Asia and what is now Alaska at least 10,000, perhaps 20,000, years ago. These were the ancestors of many American tribes, but scientists fail to agree that they were the forefathers of all New World Indians. Several theories claim many of South America's aboriginal groups came by boat across the Pacific. These may have been well established by the time decendants of other Asiatics worked their way down over thousands of years from Alaska, through Central America, and into the Andes Mountains and bordering lowlands.

At Valdivia, a few miles from Salinas, Ecuador, pottery discoveries show men lived there about 3,000 years before the birth of Christ. The oldest pottery yet discovered in this part of the New World, it resembles certain Japanese claywork of 3,000 B.C. Some archeologists think this indicates a culture established by Japanese travelers; others suspect it means only that a boatload of Japanese, because of storms and ocean currents, made an accidental landfall there and taught their type of handiwork to people already settled in the area.

Another interesting find has been made on Puná Island, in the Gulf of Guayaquil. A small bead, possibly connected with spinning, discovered in 1965 has a carved figure on it closely resembling the birdmen figures on Easter Island. These are human figures wearing bird masks but with unusually large hands and feet. The Easter Island bird-

At Amerindian Plaza in Quito, Ecuador, are busts of the most famous New World Indians—one for each country of the Organization of American States. From left to right are Tupac Kutari (Bolivia), Rumiñahui (Ecuador), and Tupac Amaru (Peru)

men carvings, it is thought, represent winners in an annual race of daring and ability. About a mile from Easter Island, Moto Nui, a rocky islet, juts up from the water. In September—which is spring, south of the equator—birds by the thousands come to this islet to nest, and Easter Islanders of old held a contest to see what man could swim to the island and return first with an unbroken egg. Strong currents and sharks as well as distance made this a difficult achievement, and the winner received a hero's honors until the next race the following spring. Since research has not yet turned up any other birdmen in South America of this exact type, it has been concluded that Easter Islanders reached Puná Island. A case might be made for the theory that some of the same people who settled on Easter Island about the time Christ was born later reached the west coast of South America. It seems more likely to some scientists that a few descendants of the original Easter Islanders accidentally reached the New World, probably between A.D. 500 and 1000, and introduced the birdman figure.

Handcrafts are not the only links between South America's western regions and Asia. An unusual type of cotton with both large and small chromosomes grows in Peru. Most wild Peruvian cotton has small chromosomes, while the typical wild cotton of Asia has large ones. Many botanists consider the Peruvian cotton that exhibits both types of chromosomes to be a hybrid between the two and another strong indication that Orientals reached South America directly in a matter of weeks rather than by the roundabout route across Alaska that took countless centuries. Men studying the travels and life histories of gourds, sweet potatoes, and maize also find evidence to indicate northwestern South America may have been settled, whether accidentally or purposefully, by families making fairly direct voyages from Asia or Pacific islands.

Indians B.C.

Because the names of early Indian groups cannot be learned from their bones or artifacts, the groups carry the names of some of their characteristics or of the sites at which discoverers located their remains. This means that some of the oldest known groups, in northern Peru and possibly southern Ecuador, are called the Huaca, since these groups built adobe buildings rather than thatch huts, and a building was a huaca. (Later, in Inca times, a huaca was a temple or else some natural object, like a mountain peak or boulder, that was worshipped.) The earliest people of the Huaca cultures may have lived 8,000 years ago but undoubtedly existed at least 3,000 years before Christ. Like other Indians who followed them in living along Peru's coastal lowland, they occupied river valleys to escape the desert conditions existing away from rivers. They survived by fishing, with some hunting and occasional gathering of a few plants. Mackerel, bonito, herring, sea bass, and various shellfish may have been among the fish they caught. Searching among various palms, algarroba, balsa, and other trees, they speared piglike peccaries, deer, tapirs, armadillos, and iguanas. Along the coast they could have taken gulls, cormorants, and pelicans. Whether or not they ate small birds, the Huaca peoples could enjoy the beauty of the North American migrants that fly south during the northern winter, such as scarlet tanagers, redstarts, and barn swallows. A local beauty is the large, sky-blue morpho butterfly.

From gathering plant foods, the people made the natural step of discovering that seeds can be sown and crops raised. Once early peoples started putting seeds in the ground, they had to become more settled if they wanted to reap the rewards of their labors. In time they became farmers, with many agricultural communities in northwestern South America probably forming after 3000 B.C. Most of the groups there carried on some agriculture by the time Christ was born. With the development of farming, the groups underwent a number of other changes from the fishing and hunting days of the Huaca and other early peoples. Being more settled, they could develop more implements and pottery, which would have been too heavy or unwieldy to carry when they roamed regularly. They developed tools for digging, crude looms for weaving, and stone-chipping implements. They fashioned tools and utensils of copper, tin, and silver, minerals abundant in the central Andes region. Because they could no longer wander away from one another in time of trouble or disagreement, they began accepting the will of leaders.

Cults and Experimenters

The Chavín, a religious cult rather than a single tribe, lived high up the mountain slopes. Chavín peoples built impressive temples and showed special respect for catlike animals in their worship. Around them in northern Peru and Ecuador lived jaguars and pumas. Perhaps some of these large cats, growing old or being wounded, attacked Chavín peoples, thereby causing the Indians to respect these animals worshipfully. Perhaps the Indians simply admired the courage, intelligence, hunting skill, and strength of these beasts. Added onto cat figures were characteristics of fish and birds. The Chavín beliefs had some influence on a great many of the peoples in what are now Ecuador and northern Peru.

At the time the Chavín peoples influenced religion, the Indians of the Andes were discovering how to make mountain slopes usable by building terraces. Irrigation helped them to survive the yearly dry season, and among their increasing number of crops they included

To keep from being clawed to pieces, a worker at a wild animal collection center along the Amazon River in Peru wears heavy gloves to handle an ocelot. This familiar creature of the mountains and jungles was once probably an object of worship of the Chavín peoples

22

various beans, squashes, maize, avocados, and peanuts. Living where there were cacti, yuccas, shrubs, and *hichu* grass rather than many palms or larger trees, the mountain people used sun-baked clay, or adobe, for building. Without doubt these people and the Chavín peoples ate meat as well as vegetable products, but they may have learned to domesticate some creatures instead of hunting every animal they ate. At least some early highland peoples tamed llamas and alpacas, which are two of the camels of the New World, as well as guinea pigs and at least one species of duck.

After the Chavín religious cult brought some uniformity among the widespread groups of northwestern South America, a trend developed toward political organization. Although most groups remained quite independent of one another, governments were often similar. Groups like the Chiripa of Bolivia, who reached their height of power perhaps three hundred years before Christ came into the world, are called Experimenters. They and peoples like them throughout the central Andes region—such as the Salinar and the Cavernas—helped bring the change from religious and cult leadership to actual government control. Of course they didn't consciously experiment with types of governments, but their trial-and-error activities look somewhat like experiments to us today. Early leaders functioned as priests first and became government officials because the priesthood put them in positions of power. In time close blood relatives banded together, and the leaders that emerged gained much of their power by being heads of large and strong families.

The Chiripa and others like them improved on arts such as boat building and road building. Their bridges crossed wider gaps and carried greater weights than those of their predecessors. They had a kind of suspension bridge, now called *mimbre*, for which the suspension cables were braided withes, or slender willow branches and twigs. They made more use of metals than their ancestors and probably also used more ornamentation, for which gold and silver served especially well. Weaving became more advanced, with human hair and cotton serving as fiber for cloth in addition to alpaca and llama wool.

Around the Chiripa lived several types of doves, hummingbirds, and finches, which flew about among dwarf willows, alders, and bunch grass. Today, a mustard-colored finch serves, like the robin in North America, as a sign that spring is arriving. Some of the doves and hummingbirds go unseen by most highland residents today, yet a long dry spell may bring even the rarest ones to fountains in city parks. Hummingbirds have always been especially important for fertilizing the strange *Puya raimondii* plant of high and rocky places. A bromeliad having its root system growing in the open air instead of in the ground and a relative of the pineapple, this plant develops so slowly that it may take a century to reach a height of ten feet. The dark, grayish-green leaves are long and narrow, reaching lengths of three to four feet. They grow in a thick cluster about the plant's stem, and as the old ones die, they droop down around the trunk and help the plant retain moisture. About every five years a flower stalk stretches fifteen feet above the trunk and begins to bloom from the bottom up between October and December. The seed pods that follow the blooms send forth hundreds of thousands of seeds from each plant, but probably only one in a million gets a chance to grow, so Bolivia is in no danger of being overrun by this bromeliad.

Where the Experimenter Indians lived on the high plateaus, they had the wind for a constant companion. Those settling in deep valleys escaped the winds, and many of them escaped insect pests as well. Along the coasts mosquitoes, sandflies, fleas, and other insects not only bothered humans by biting but transmitted serious diseases to them. Yellow fever, malaria, plague, and typhus killed white men when they reached the area and must have affected the early Indian populations. Of course, the white men may have brought some of the diseases with them. Many valleys have always been free of the insect carriers of these diseases and also of vampire bats. While the winged mammals don't kill people by syphoning off all their blood, a rabies infection may be transmitted by a vampire bite.

The Chiripa and other Experimenters probably never scaled the highest points of the Andes around them, nor did the Indians who lived later. The loftiest peak in Peru, that of Mt. Huascarán, reaches 22,205 feet. This is not much shorter than Argentina's Mt. Aconcagua, which at 22,889 feet is South America's high point. Bolivia boasts a mountain

—Illampú—stretching 21,489 feet above sea level, while Ecuador reaches to 20,561 feet with Mt. Chimborazo. All three countries have a number of mountains that wear snow mantles the year round, and Ecuador can claim the only glacier in the world flowing across the equator. This ice river oozes down Cayambe, a volcanic peak, to cross the zero parallel 19,000 feet above sea level.

In Christian Times

From the time of the Experimenters on, powerful groups of Indians dominated the regions in which they lived. Some of these were the Nazca toward the south and the Mochica farther north. They started to develop at least a century before Christ was born but probably grew strongest six hundred years later. Often called Mastercraftsmen, they

A ritual is performed before a stone gate of the Tiahuanaco period. This particular one is called the Sun Gate by modern scientists who think it shows the Inca Sun God surrounded by his warriors. It was built after the Incas took over the Tiahuanaco site from earlier peoples

advanced agriculture, pottery, implement-making, and weaving. For them, hunting of wild game ceased to be a necessity (since they kept large herds of llamas and alpacas as well as guinea pigs for slaughter) and became a sport. Families lived close together, forming villages and at times cities. But their settlements could hardly compare in size and complexity to some soon to follow. Ruins of one of the most noteworthy of these later settlements can still be seen at Tiahuanaco, Bolivia. The Nazca groups came under the influence of the Tiahuanacans and gradually lost their separate identity.

Tiahuanaco stands in one of the most interesting regions of the altiplano. The countryside here lies a little more than two miles above sea level and presents desertlike conditions. Yet only a dozen miles away is an abundance of water—Lake Titicaca. The highest important and navigable lake in the world, Titicaca straddles the border between Peru and Bolivia. With a length of 138 miles, a width of 69, and an area of 3,200 square miles, it is the second largest lake in South America (Venezuela's Maracaibo is larger). Much of its water comes from mountains over 20,000 feet high to the north and east. At the time the Tiahuanaco civilization flourished, Lake Titicaca supplied the water the people needed, and the city may even have stood on an island in the lake. The Indians were probably unaware when they first built there that the lake shrank a little each year and would gradually withdraw from their settlement.

Some of the ruins at Tiahuanaco show Indians lived there during the first centuries of the Christian era, but the people probably became really powerful eight or nine hundred years later. The Tiahuanacan peoples built large temples, entered by massive gates on which they carved a variety of figures. A sun-god figure shows they honored the sun, but they also depicted pumas, condors, and serpents. Modern-day scientists think the large temple area Puma Punco ("Door of the Puma") served as a seat of justice. This indicates Tiahuanaco stood as the capital of a wide-spreading kingdom. The peoples of this city spread their government and culture through the central Andes partly by conquest, though religion more than military exploits held their groups together.

A Power Group in the Lowlands

While the Tiahuanacans spread their influence on the altiplano, the Chimus became powerful in the northern coastal lowlands and the Chinchas reigned to the south. The Chimus, especially, developed a great empire, relying on warfare to bring their ways to weaker peoples. They carried their rule across the lowlands and into the mountains, absorbing the Mochica culture among others. While the Tiahuanacans remained strong, they held the Chimus back from the Titicaca area, but by A.D. 1000 the Tiahuanacan culture had reached its peak. The Chimus gained strength as the Tiahuanacans lost it; no one today knows how much territory fell under the control of the Chimus. According to some archeologists, the Chimu kingdom eventually exceeded that of the Tiahuanacans, yet other scientists suspect it was smaller. In any case it controlled nearly fifty groups of people and covered thousands of square miles, perhaps the northern half of Peru, around A.D. 1200. Its capital, Chan Chan, dwarfed Tiahuanaco.

As finances permit today, Peruvian and other archeologists dig into the site of Chan Chan, near Trujillo, Peru, to restore walls of temples and houses. They know the city covered eleven square miles—half the size of New York City's Manhattan Island—and housed a population of about 250,000. The people made all structures of adobe, the natural building material of Peru's coastal desert. This explains why Tiahuanaco, partly built of stone, has stood weathering better than Chan Chan. In some ancient languages *chan* means "snake," while in others it stands for "sun," and scientists disagree as to the meaning of the city's name. The information given out by Peruvian authorities favors the sun interpretation. Yet the moon rather than the sun was probably the leading god of the people. None of the Indian groups ruled from Chan Chan went by the name Chimu. Instead, the ruler himself received the grand title of Great Chimu, so all peoples under him became known as the Chimus.

The Chimus built Chan Chan on raised ground, though little of the land along Peru's coast at Trujillo reaches any notable height. Besides houses and temples, they had special ceremonial grounds, pools in which the higher officials could swim or soak to escape the heat of the

All of Chan Chan was walled off into sections, and each section was occupied by a family group. Below is the Temple of the Dragon, also part of the great Chimu Indian city. In addition to having some religious· significance, the temple served as a granary

coast, and well-planned streets. Some houses had windows—openings left high up in the walls—but others received ventilation through doors and roofs. Frames of cane in the ceiling could be opened to let air enter or escape, while plugs of straw and thatch closed the spaces during a storm. The poor people closed the spaces left for doors by hanging woven reed mats over them, while well-to-do people and officials draped furs in their doorways. Officials had cane chairs, some with handles so they became litters that could be carried through the streets. Good quality cloth went into the Chimu breechcloths, wraparound skirts, and slipover shirts, which were made both of wool and cotton and decorated with fish and fowl designs. As sheep didn't reach the continent until later, when the Spanish conquistadors arrived, the wool at this time came from the small camels of the highlands—llamas, alpacas, and possibly vicuñas. The clothes a person wore usually distinguished his work and rank in community life from those of his neighbors. Feathers on his costume indicated a man held high office as a rule.

Indian life changed considerably during the time of the Chimus. Before, people had occupied villages or had even lived in small family groups apart from regular settlements. But the Chimu period brought unrest and warfare, until families banded together for protection. Not only did Chan Chan grow huge, but towns sprang up throughout Chimu territory while separate individual dwellings disappeared. Every town had a high wall, with larger towns being divided into smaller areas by protective walls inside the outer ones. Chan Chan itself consisted of ten large units, each one walled in and each one broken down by additional interior walls. The interior walls may have separated family groups from one another. Some walls lacked decoration, but those for special courts or temples had a variety of designs worked into the clay. Fish, birds, and squirrel-like animals occurred repeatedly throughout Chimu settlements.

During the Chimu period the Indians learned to process ores better than before and discovered how to make bronze from tin and copper. The common people used what bronze they could obtain for needles and the tips of digging sticks, but much of the production went to make war clubs and knives for warriors. Several metals, especially

29

gold and silver, served to make earrings, beads, necklaces, and dishes. The common people among the Chimus, unable to have decorations and utensils of valuable metals, used bone, shell, and colored rocks. The Chimus adopted some cultural features from the Mochicas, including ear plugs and possibly the nose and lip plugs of those people. Undoubtedly they borrowed other ways of life from other peoples who fell under their domination. In turn they passed much of their knowledge and some ways of life on when they fell to a stronger group, the Incas.

Jungle Peoples and Animals

The dominating groups, from the early Huacas to the Incas, lived along the coasts and in the mountains. Except for the Incas they apparently had little contact with the peoples scattered through the *montaña* (foothills) and rain forest on the east side of the Andes. Here the groups moved about more, and so found huts of palm poles and thatch more practical than buildings of stone or adobe. They never banded together in large enough communities to build great temples, and only a few, such as the Mojo of eastern Bolivia, had settlements that might

A witch doctor of the Yagua tribe shows how to shoot a blowgun. Indians in grass skirts like this were mistaken for women warriors by the early Spanish explorers and caused the Amazon to receive its name

be called towns. They made some pottery, when their small villages became permanent, and knew how to weave but often dressed in plant materials if they wore clothes at all. Clothing served to protect them from insects and rain, as temperatures always remained high, never dropping into the forties or below as it does regularly in the mountain areas. Most of the jungle groups lived beside or near waterways, which provided them with fish, iguanas, caymans, ducks, and egrets to eat. Some people produced poisons from plants and threw these into the rivers to kill fish, a highly wasteful way of gathering food since the poison killed those too small to use and many of the dead fish floated off with the current. The Mojos farmed around their settlements, raising maize, sweet potatoes, beans, peanuts, squash, and papayas. Various Indian groups became expert shots with blowguns from which they expelled poisoned darts. With a blowgun a man of steady aim could hit a hummingbird dozens of yards away. Of course, some hummingbirds of the rain forest reach lengths of five inches. The Indians more often shot tropical orioles, parrots, and toucans, made easily visible by bright colors and medium to large size. These Indians also ate howler and other monkeys, as their descendants still do today.

As hunters slipped among cedar, mahogany, ebony, balsam, and palm trees and thousands of smaller plants, they produced no noise on the jungle floor, made springy by decaying leaves. The beauty of large butterflies or of orchids and other epiphytes (air plants) hardly turned their attention from their purpose. In any tree a man might discover a sloth, while an ocelot sometimes whisked across a slight clearing. Even geckoes could serve as food if a man's family grew hungry enough to eat small lizards. As he hunted, the man watched for such dangerous snakes as the poisonous bushmaster and fer-de-lance. These have always been the two most feared creatures of the tropical jungles, though they probably cause few deaths. Today even explorers armed with snakebite serum fear the bushmaster. It may reach a length of twelve feet, and as the world's largest viper, pours a great quantity of venom into anything it bites. Its long fangs discharge the poison deep in the victim's body, where it starts taking immediate effect, so a counteracting serum may work too slowly to save any person who gets struck by a bushmaster.

Fer-de-lances, which are distant relatives of rattlesnakes but without rattles, and bushmasters hunt at night. The ancient Indians were usually safely home in hammocks when these snakes appeared and thereby avoided them.

Anacondas may be more dangerous than the poisonous snakes because they occasionally attack without reason. These huge constrictors loop around their prey and squeeze it until it suffocates. They grow to a length of nearly thirty feet, but in spite of their size they go undiscovered much of the time because of living in the tropical rivers. All the jungle people along the Amazon tell stories of anacondas suddenly surfacing like sea monsters to snatch people out of canoes. Cases where such events have actually been proven true are so rare that most authorities on snakes consider these to be colorful tall tales designed to excite or frighten listeners. Anacondas also go by the name river boas, indicating they are related to smaller constrictors of the same area, such as the tree and rainbow boas.

People of the jungles have often met other dangerous animals besides snakes. Scorpions and tarantulas thrive in the tropical climate, and while their stings and bites may not kill, they can make a man mighty sick. They are more of a danger to small children, whose bodies lack the strength to counteract the poison. Mosquitoes find numberless places to breed in the jungle, but through the course of centuries, most of the Indians have developed a resistance to the diseases these pests carry. Modern-day spraying around settled areas now helps keep small winged enemies under control to a large degree. However, if he waded into a river to fish, a man might step on an electric eel or be attacked by piranhas. Electric eels of the Amazon, relatives of catfishes rather than of true eels, can paralyze a man with a discharge of up to six hundred volts. Piranha fish have razor-sharp teeth and easily bite off toes or strip the flesh from a man's leg. They always travel in schools, and a drop of blood in the water attracts them from considerable distances. With so many creatures to watch out for, the ancient Indians probably never thought of swarms of cockroaches and crickets as pests.

Savages and Headhunters

Of far more danger than all the animals of the jungle were the people themselves. The Yuqui Indians remain fierce down to modern times, keeping other Indians in prehistoric days and white men more recently from moving into certain areas of northeastern Bolivia. At one time within recent decades some Bolivian officials proposed wiping them out, something the United Nations would never permit if it could help it. Since their first contacts with white men, the Yuqui have been greatly reduced in numbers from natural causes, and missionary doctors and UN workers with modern medicines cannot approach them to help them fight disease. Nature itself has about wiped them out by now.

In Ecuador one of the wildest groups has been the Aucas. Living on the south side of the Napo River, they still kill people who enter their territory. Missionaries have lived among them within the past fifteen years, only to be unaccountably massacred after seeming to win their respect and friendship. Hunters who stray into their region may pass unharmed or may be speared on sight. The Aucas go naked but never unarmed. They carry wooden spears, which prove more deadly than they sound since they are made of the iron-hard chonta palm. The northern boundary of these Indians, Río Napo, flows from 19,000 feet high on Mt. Cotopaxi across northeastern Ecuador. For a short distance

Near Iquitos, Peru, the closely related Campa and Aguaruna tribes are now tourist attractions. A few youngsters still dress in traditional straw clothing, paint their bodies with plant juices, and wear decorations of animal bones and skins around their foreheads, necks, arms, or legs

it forms the boundary between Ecuador and Peru before entering Peru and serving as a major tributary of the Amazon. Large ships can navigate the Napo, but they no longer come up river as far as Ecuador because of a border dispute between this country and Peru.

Though the Aucas have not been tamed, the once-fierce Jivaros have responded to missionary teachings. They may still practice animism (belief in the existence of spirits within natural objects such as rocks and trees), but they have given up killing enemies and shrinking their heads. The basis for their headhunting was an ancient legend, which made them feel they needed to take heads as an act of self-preservation. The legend says that one day, ages before white men came and gave them the name Jivaros, some of their people were swimming at the foot of a mountain. A huge snake, perhaps an enormous ancestor of today's anaconda, came down the slopes and swallowed them before they could get away. Warriors, rushing to the lake on hearing the screams of the swimmers, caught the serpent and cut off its head. For fear the huge head might still swallow other people, they shrank it, and from then on the Jivaros continued to shrink heads of their enemies to rid them of any evil powers they might possess. In time they came to believe they secured an enemy's prowess when they took his head.

They had many enemies in addition to men they fought in time of war. Whenever a person died, even from obvious causes such as drowning, falling, or being attacked by a wounded jaguar, the Jivaros felt an enemy's evil spell had been at work. They consulted their witch doctors, who took narcotics to put themselves in a trance from which they always recovered knowing the identity of the guilty person. (It is easy to imagine what happened to anybody unfortunate enough to attract the displeasure of a witch doctor.) The Jivaros quickly prepared to bring the guilty party to justice, which ended with his head being shrunk and the lips and eyes of the *tsanza,* or miniaturized head, being sewed shut or plugged up with wooden slivers.

To have heads to sell to tourists, the Jivaros now buy them from morgues and shrink them. Since the upper Amazon region has become easily accessible because of airplanes and motorboats, the Jivaros and

Dressed in a ceremonial costume of the type used by the Yagua Indians for centuries, a young man of the tribe plays on a tribal drum. The instrument once called boys of twelve or thirteen to the ceremony that would give them the right to consider themselves men. Costumes were to make them think they were being tested by spirits rather than by men of their tribe

surrounding tribes serve as tourist attractions. Among the best-known of these jungle groups are the Yaguas, who live in the region of Iquitos, Peru. Hunting with blowguns, farming, and sleeping in hammocks, they live somewhat as their ancestors did. But they have adopted a new type of house. Before white men reached them, they lived in houses that seemed to be all roof. The front and back were triangles to support the roof of palm leaves woven through slender poles, and the roof slanted down on either side from a central ridge to come to rest on the ground. This house flooded easily and was accessible to all creatures creeping and crawling on the ground. Today, the Yaguas live in stick and thatch houses held a few feet above the ground by stilts.

Islands of Special Interest

While the sierra and coast supported heavy populations by the time white men reached the New World, the jungle has always remained thinly settled. Even today, hundreds of square miles seldom see an intruder as far as anyone knows. The only areas of these countries that have fewer occupants than the jungle are the offshore islands. Bolivia has no islands to claim, but various points of rock reach above sea level off the coasts of Peru and Ecuador. Most of these support bird life, seals, and walruses rather than human beings. Because of the hundreds of thousands of cormorants, gulls, and other sea birds that nest on them, the islands are blanketed with droppings which make excellent fertilizer. Peruvians call the accumulation of droppings *guano,* which means "dung," and the word has been accepted into the English language. Pinpoints of land such as the Chincha Islands have economic value to Peru because of the use of guano for fertilizer.

Ecuador, too, possesses guano islands, but of far more importance is the Archipiélago de Colón, commonly known as the Galápagos Islands. Claimed by Ecuador in 1832, these lie across the equator 650 miles west of Ecuador and have an area (2,966 square miles) larger than the state of Delaware. Though they support a few villages, they are mostly interesting because of the outposts on them at which scientists study the unusual animal life. Charles Darwin called attention to the islands and their animals after he visited the archipelago in 1835. At that time they still went by the name Enchanted Islands, a name given them by their discoverer, Tomás de Berlanga, in 1535. Darwin was delighted to find animals living practically free of human influence and was especially impressed to discover that each of the twenty major islands had a species of turtle peculiarly its own. This interest in shelled reptiles led to the islands being called the Galápagos, which means "tortoises," and helped Darwin develop his theories of evolution. Though a turtle of one island had differences from those of the other islands, similarities made him suspect the reptiles could have had a common ancestor. He wrote in his *Journal* that the Galápagos Islands played a role in his views as expressed in 1859 when he published *The Origin of Species*. He also visited Peru, where he undoubtedly took an interest in the native peoples as well as in the reptiles, birds, mammals, and plant life there. The Indians he would have seen the most of were the Quechuas, who are modern-day Incas, an Indian civilization that has been the subject of many legends and archeological expeditions.

Children of the Sun

Because the Incas developed a remarkable civilization and controlled lands from Colombia to central Chile, they receive credit for the accomplishments of people who came before them. Llamas, which may have resulted from crossing alpacas with vicuñas, as well as alpacas had been domesticated before the time of the Incas. But earlier peoples had used these animals mainly for wool and food, while the Incas employed them to carry loads as well. In agriculture the Incas probably learned of terracing and irrigation from earlier peoples but went far beyond their predecessors in using the knowledge. Several people before the Incas built great cities and buildings. Yet in a few hundred years the Incas accomplished so much with what they learned from older cultures and through their own efforts that they built an empire quite surpassing anything before their time in the central Andes.

Most peoples within the Inca empire had no idea they descended from earlier peoples. For all their developments, the Incas never produced a written language, nor had their predecessors. Priests and other high officials remembered what they could of Inca history, showing no interest in the backgrounds of peoples forced into the empire. Certain men served as storytellers, repeating legends the priests taught them until all peoples in the realm became "brainwashed" and knew only the accepted "facts."

A descendant of the Incas spins thread as she goes to market carrying her youngest child on her back

For centuries fishermen on Lake Titicaca have built distinctively shaped boats of reeds since the high mountains lack trees for wood

Legends versus Science

According to the approved view, the Sun, Father of the Incas, created a new race of people to be rulers of the Andean region. By his trusted and most feared minister, Lightning, the Sun sent a man and a woman to an island in Lake Titicaca. Tourists today visit this Sun Island, but about the only Incan remains they now see are terraces for agriculture and a flight of steps. The first man created by the Sun married the woman, though she was his sister, and every leader following the first man married a sister because no other woman had sufficient royal blood to be his wife. The Sun Father, *Inti*, provided the man, Manco Capac, with a rod of gold for testing the land over which he traveled. When he found soil so loose the golden shaft sank from sight in it, the man had orders to found his capital, and legend says such land awaited him where Cuzco, Peru, now stands. Manco Capac and his sister-wife,

Mama Ocllo, taught the local people to farm, weave, and worship the Sun, thus starting the "Children of the Sun" race. More likely, a warlike family began conquering neighbors in the early centuries of the Christian era. By the fifteenth century a kingdom had been established, which a few dynamic leaders then extended into a huge empire.

Supposedly, Manco Capac called his capital Cuzco—which can be translated "navel"—because it was to be the center of his realm, and took Inca, which may mean "Son of the Sun" or possibly just "lord," for his own title. All rulers following him carried the same title, so white men referred to groups under these leaders as the Incas' people, and eventually, the Incas. One large segment of the Incas came to be called Quechuas. Originally, it is thought, people living in valleys called themselves the *keshwa*. When the Spanish arrived they spelled this word *Quechua* and used it to mean the main Inca language. In the twentieth century, careless usage applied Quechua to the people who spoke the language as well as to the tongue itself. Large numbers of people on the altiplano who spoke another language were called Aymara, and Quechua

Sun Island in Lake Titicaca is famous among the Inca Indians as the legendary birthplace of their race

and Aymara remain the two major tongues and the two main groups of people of the central Andes today.

The Capital

If one believes the ancient legends, Cuzco in about 1250 became a great city overnight. Archeologists say it grew gradually and developed on the foundations of older communities. At its heart stood a huge square, sacred to the Inca and the royal family but "off limits" to the common people. The commoners held their gatherings and festivals in *Cusi Pata* ("Square of Happiness"), a short distance north of the main square. The empire grew to include twelve provinces, and each of these was represented by one of Cuzco's twelve sections. Within each section the people dressed like their relatives out in the provinces, making a city of colorful contrasts. Four roads ran from the capital to connect it with the areas it controlled. Various buildings and temples within the city served special purposes, with the Temple of the Sun being most important, most sacred, and most wealthy. The Incas

42

coated or decorated every part of this temple with gold—"tears of the Sun"—and used precious stones, such as emeralds, for specials effects. When the Spanish captured the Incas, they "mined" the temple for every ounce of its precious materials. In time Catholic priests built the monastery of Santo Domingo on the temple's foundations, but in the late 1960s efforts to restore some of the original building progressed leisurely. Other ruins in and around Cuzco also remind present-day visitors of the city's Inca heritage. Tambomachay, home of the Inca, and Sacsahuamán and Puca-Pucará, forts, attract thousands of visitors annually.

Incas at Home

The ordinary people lived in simple rectangular houses, built of mud in the highlands and of sticks or adobe toward the coast. Thatch for the roofs came from whatever local grasses and reeds proved abundant. Especially in the mountains the only openings were low doors which helped keep heat in and cold out. A practical people, these Indians built their homes on hillsides and other places ill-suited to agriculture. This left the level land and good soil for farming, though the Incas knew how to improve the land with nitrogen-rich bird guano from the coastal islands. A family of several people lived in one room, but as sons married and the family unit grew, a partition might be put up to divide the house in two. A family's guinea pigs shared the house, but llamas and alpacas faced the weather outside. Government regulations forbade household decorations to the common people, but they could sleep on a llama skin and pull part of it over themselves as a blanket against the cold. An official enjoyed the privilege of spreading his llama skin over a platform of grass. Not even the Inca had a real bed but slept on a sort of mattress on the floor.

Though she couldn't beautify her home, a woman could have some personal adornment and often wore a large-headed silver *topu* to pin her shawl about her shoulders. People with beads, bracelets, and earplugs for the slits in their earlobes ranked above the common people. Clothing had a practical purpose, to protect the body, so people in the warm regions went without garments unless insects forced them to protect the more sensitive areas. Cotton served for clothing in the

43

lowlands, while llama and alpaca wool gave more warmth for the mountains. Only people of high rank could wear vicuña wool. Women in the highlands wore long sacklike tunics with side slits for free leg movement. Around their waists they had belts, and over their shoulders shawls. Men wore shorter shirtlike tunics, breechcloths, and blanketlike capes. Much of the time the people went barefoot, though they could use sandals. Men and women working on steep slopes regularly wore short sandals which left their toes sticking out in front to help them get a toehold on the rocky soil as they climbed. All the women spun and wove for the community. Many garments they made went into a general warehouse and from time to time, such as when he married, a person was granted clothing from this supply.

The common people lived in family groups—*ayllus*—which were the basic units of society. Great numbers of them farmed, producing crops for community granaries. This means the Inca society was partially communistic, but community control didn't extend to everything. A family owned its house, and a woman's cooking jars and weaving implements belonged to her. But officials kept much of each *ayllus'* goods and produce in community storehouses against times of emergency. A person who failed to work might be refused food from the

Indian women still perform the same tasks as their ancestors, but they have moved out from the community to the market place for more profit

granaries, which meant most people were reasonably industrious. The stores provided sun-dried llama meat, from the slaughter of young animals, since those over two or three years of age have bitter flesh. Maize and potatoes were the main vegetables, supplemented by tomatoes (another vegetable native to the Andes), squash, sweet potatoes, various beans, lupines (edible peas), hot peppers, and manioc. From maize the Incas fermented *chicha,* a strong drink forbidden to them except during festivals. Most Indians on the altiplano still drink *chicha* today, but now their finances rather than officials are all that stand in their way of getting drunk whenever they like. Land belonged to the empire—as tradition put it, to the Sun. No man could accumulate property and rise above others of his class. The three classes were the royalty, or relatives of the emperors; the nobility, made up of high officials and their relatives; and the commoners.

Runners and City Builders

From time to time the Inca traveled through his provinces, carried in a litter and wearing clothes of exquisite workmanship and beauty. He could reach almost any corner of his realm at any time of year, for the Incas built about ten thousand miles of stone-paved or adobe roads. The longest stretch reached from Cuzco through Quitu (now Quito, Ecuador) and into Colombia. Runners covered these roads in relays, carrying messages as fast as man could race. Every two to four miles small houses offered shelter to the *chasquis,* as runners were known. When a messenger came dashing toward a waiting post, another *chasqui* ran out to meet him. They raced side by side until the first runner had stated his message and the second man memorized it. Or the first man might hand the second one a quipu, a rope from which hung smaller cords of various colors, some of which might be knotted. The colors and knots all had special meanings and so provided a message. The quipu also served as a counting device, which was probably its original and main function. Once a message had passed from one *chasqui* to another, the first runner stopped and rested at the waiting post, where he found food.

Workmen of special skill built remarkable structures for the empire. Without the aid of cement or even of clay to serve as mortar, they set stone on stone so perfectly that some of their handiwork still stands today. When the conquistadors arrived, they destroyed many of the fine buildings through greed for riches or because the structures represented a pagan religion. But persistent rumors down to modern times tell of hidden cities never discovered by the Spaniards. In the early years of the twentieth century Hiram Bingham, a professor at Yale University, searched among the peaks of Peru to find such cities. In 1911 he followed the Urubamba River as it flows north of Cuzco, a region supposedly crawling with poisonous snakes. He and a few assistants scrambled up a 2,000-foot slope, "a good part of the distance . . . on all fours, sometimes holding on by our fingertips," to reach a small peak between two higher ones. There he found a family of Indian farmers and the well-preserved ruins of Machu Picchu. Bingham's discovery opened to the world one of the greatest tourist attractions of

A panorama of Machu Picchu, fortress city of the ancient Incas and one of their last strongholds after the Spanish conquest, located about fifty miles northwest of Cuzco

Tourists to Machu Picchu discover the home of Indian mountain-dwellers who preserve much of their ancient heritage

South America. After visiting it, Pablo Neruda, Chile's greatest modern poet, wrote his best-known work, *The Heights of Machu Picchu.* At Machu Picchu, you can see the remaining walls of houses, granaries, and temples, in addition to tier on tier of 10-foot high terraces. How the Inca workmen handled the large stones they used remains a mystery, but some system must have existed for levering, hauling, or heaving the heavy building blocks into place. Today visitors accustomed to low altitudes may gasp for breath because the air, a mile and a half high, contains less oxygen than air near sea level. Yet the Incas accomplished amazing feats requiring great physical effort and lived sometimes for more than eighty years. The Incan year, though it started a month earlier than our year, was based on the position of the sun and so had the same length as the modern year.

47

Distributing the Work

We know some Incas enjoyed long lives because of regulations governing their work. The rules excused men between eighty and a hundred years of age from labor. Those under eighty but over fifty also escaped heavy duty, though they herded the llamas and tended to light tasks. The real workers, runners, soldiers, and other people needing to put forth great effort fell in the twenty-five-to-fifty-year age group, while men under twenty-five still passed as young people and weren't expected to do a grown man's work. Sick, infirm, and injured people avoided regular work loads and might even be taken to special places for their health. The Inca Indians had playgrounds and resort areas the same as we do today. When they found a valley where the climate was good, they built houses in which sick people could rest and recover from their illnesses. The royalty and nobility had palaces in some of these vales, made especially beautiful with well-tended gardens and comfortable with pools for both bathing and swimming.

The Empire Spreads

The Incas left some of the rain forest peoples out of their empire, which may mean they found the groups too small and scattered to be welded into the *ayllus* (family) system. But the mountain and coastal Indians from southern Colombia to central Chile fell before Inca soldiers. Below central Chile the fierce Mapuche Indians, clever at jungle warfare, kept the "Children of the Sun" from advancing farther south. Most of the empire developed after 1438, when Pachacuti probably came to power. Disliked by his father, this royal son seemed to have small chance of becoming Inca until he led soldiers to a great, bloody victory. The son who followed him about 1471, Topa Inca, continued the program of conquests started by Pachacuti, and was in turn succeeded by a warlike son, Huayna Capac, about 1493. Each Inca chose the son who would succeed him, for rule didn't necessarily go to the eldest. Huayna Capac either died before picking his successor or else felt the empire had grown too large for one man to handle. He left the northern part to Atahualpa, his favorite son, and the rest to Huáscar,

Quito, Ecuador, as it now looks, five centuries after the Inca Empire. The Presidential Palace dominates one side of Quito's Plaza de la Independencia, and another famous landmark, the Cathedral, stands at right angles to the palace

the legitimate heir. Whatever these half-brothers thought of each other before, they became enemies at this point.

Living in Quitu, Atahualpa probably felt exiled from the traditional capital, Cuzco, where Huáscar held control. Trouble existed between the two sections of the empire for a few years before finally leading to open warfare. It came at the worst possible moment, for Francisco Pizarro and his small band of followers had already landed on the shores of Peru. At this time part of the Inca armies were far away. Having heard of island civilizations in the Pacific, Huayna Capac had sent thousands of soldiers, on balsa rafts, to conquer them. From visiting the guano islands and possibly others, the Incas knew something of the strong current that runs along the coast of Peru. This river in the ocean, now called the Humboldt, or the Peru, Current, comes across the South Pacific and turns north along the coast of Chile. It flows past

Peru and is one of the reasons the coast of Peru gets little rain. This cold current chills the air above it and causes moisture to fall before reaching the shoreline. Near southern Ecuador the Humboldt Current meets another ocean river, an equatorial current, coming down from the north and they both turn out to sea again. The Incas either understood or suspected they could reach distant islands by riding the currents.

White Man with Beard

Old stories may have helped to guide them. One legend tells of a god with a white skin and a beard named Kon Tiki who lived by Lake Titicaca. When his city fell to invading Indians, he fled to the coast where his followers built balsa rafts on which they sailed into the sunset. In the twentieth century, scientists have experimented to show that South Americans, possibly of a white race later extinct in the New World, could have floated west and settled the Polynesian islands. Thor Heyerdahl of Norway prepared an expedition of five men besides himself to attempt to sail by raft from Peru to Polynesia. With nine balsa logs roped together for a base and other logs crossed over them to hold a platform of bamboo, they had a raft similar to those shown in old Spanish drawings. On this they added a cabin of bamboo into which all of them could barely squeeze at once. The raft received an official name, Kon Tiki, on April 27, 1947, and headed out to sea behind a tugboat the next day. When they cut loose from the tug on April 29, the six men faced one of the great adventures of modern scientific exploration.

At the very start, the elements seemed to attack the Kon Tiki. Not yet a week away from Callao, the port for Lima, the expedition faced giant waves and roaring winds. The logs and their lashings creaked and squeaked but, contrary to predictions made by seamen on shore, the vessel held together. A variety of other frightening times came later. One day a large octopus surfaced near the raft and on another occasion a huge turtle came close. Especially startling, a fish resembling a snake leaped into the vessel one dark night and writhed about among the men, who had been asleep in the cabin, until they finally caught it. Later they learned it was a snake mackerel, a knife-toothed fish of which only skeletons had ever been seen before by men. Heyerdahl and his companions caught sharks for food, but a whale shark proved alarming since it is the world's biggest fish and could have capsized the raft. Also frightening, a school of great whales, which are mammals rather than fish, swam about the Kon Tiki. If one had risen under it or had leaped onto it (some whales leap like dolphins), the raft might well have broken apart. But the raft and all six men escaped the dangers of the Pacific and after 101 days landed safely, though with difficulties, on a small uninhabited island. It proved to be part of the Raroia Reef in the Tuamotu Archipelago, about 150 miles north of Tahiti. The Kon Tiki Expedition didn't prove that men from South America sailed to the South Pacific and settled the Polynesian islands. It did prove such a thing could be possible, but most scientists today doubt that it really happened, and the origin of the original Polynesian peoples remains a mystery. It is just possible they were briefly made a part of the widespread Inca empire by the soldiers of Huayna Capac.

Spanish Colonies

During the last years of Inca Huayna Capac's reign, white men arrived in western South America. To the Indian farmers they encountered along the coast they contributed measles, smallpox, and other diseases that quickly spread, since the local peoples had no natural resistance to them. When Huayna Capac died, in 1525 or 1527, it may have been from measles. His sudden death might account for his leaving the empire in the hands of two sons. Perhaps he intended to chose between them but never got the chance. At the time of his death he was in Quitu using it as a base for conquests in the north. Atahualpa, whose mother was a Quitu princess, immediately took command of the army there. A few years of "cold war" took place before Atahualpa and his half-brother Huáscar came to open battle. While they needled one another, the white men who had reached the shores of Peru returned to Panama with stories of Inca officials wearing gold ornaments. Hearing these tales, Francisco Pizarro dreamed of gaining a fortune and a title. The son of an unwed peasant woman, Pizarro had grown up in Spain tending pigs. The one thing he wanted more than anything else was to make people call him marquis.

Though some historians rate Pizarro as a mediocre leader compared to other conquistadors, he must have had an "agile tongue." He convinced Diego de Almagro, another common soldier, and more than a hundred men to join him in seeking the Kingdom of Gold. Later, when one unsuccessful attempt to reach Peru left them needing more money, he talked Fernando de Luque, a priest in Panama, into taking over

An historic landmark of Arequipa, Peru, is the Jesuit Church built in the 1600s with an ornate Plateresque entrance

financial affairs for them. Finally reaching what is now Ecuador in 1526, Pizarro faced a mutiny. He refused to give up and with about a dozen of his original men landed in Peru the next year. There he collected enough gold to prove it awaited the men willing to fight for it. Unable to get further help in Panama, he went to Spain for money and permission to conquer the Kingdom of Gold. At this point his friendship with Almagro lessened, as the Spanish court treated Pizarro as the superior of the two. With fewer than two hundred soldiers and about forty horses, Pizarro, in 1531, landed along the Gulf of Guayaquil, where he was later joined by groups under Hernando de Soto and Sebastián de Belalcázar (or Benalcázar). Here they acquired news of the civil war between Atahualpa and Huáscar and realized they must march inland to conquer the land.

Atahualpa's Rise and Fall

The first open battles between Atahualpa and his half-brother took place in 1530 south of Quitu. As the legitimate heir of Huayna Capac, Huáscar undoubtedly felt the Sun favored him and would bring victory to his forces. But Atahualpa's army drove back the men who came to unseat him. Atahualpa continued victorious and forced Huáscar himself to start north two years later to lead his troops in person. Before going far he met Atahualpa's trusted general Challcuchima and in the battle that occurred was taken prisoner. This immediately revealed one of the weaknesses of the Inca system. All Inca peoples depended on leadership. With Huáscar captured, his army of thousands of men felt abandoned, and they fled. Huáscar's captors threw him into prison in Cuzco while his half-brother decided what to do with him.

Atahualpa did not take part in the battle, for he had stopped to soak in the steaming sulfur baths of Cajamarca, about a hundred miles inland from the old Chimu capital Chan Chan. Though word of Huáscar's capture pleased him, runners from the northwest brought disquieting word of bearded white men approaching. Pizarro had given up waiting for Almagro to bring additional soldiers and was struggling toward Cajamarca. With a simple order, the new leader of the whole Inca empire could have ended Pizarro's dreams of riches and glory. But

54

Atahualpa waited. Perhaps he thought these white men, like the others who had reached Peru a few years before, would depart soon and peacefully. He let the Spaniards pass one easily defended site after another without interference. The farther he went, the bolder Pizarro became. The actions of the Indians told him they mistook him for a god because of his fair skin and beard. All Inca Indians were dark and had faces free of hair. Having never seen horses before, the Indians feared them, and many felt a man on a horse was all one dreadful animal. The Incas agreed to accept the leadership of Jesus Christ and the king of Spain, having no idea what this meant, and let the conquistadors pass. After nearly two months Pizarro reached Cajamarca with about 150 men, perhaps 30 of them mounted. He had left small units along the way to assist him in case retreat became necessary. The city stood deserted. This appeared to be an evil omen until a messenger came from Atahualpa, camped four miles away, to say the houses had been left at the disposal of the visitors.

In his camp Atahualpa had about 30,000 soldiers. Such frightening odds against him failed to panic Pizarro. From past experience he knew the peoples of South America had no knowledge of firearms and usually fled before them, thinking they represented captive lightning. He also knew they could be as trusting as children on occasion. He arranged a meeting with Atahualpa in the central square of Cajamarca, letting the Inca think he would be unarmed. He hid his men in the buildings around the square, where they waited with a few cannon dragged all the way from the coast as well as their small guns. When the Inca arrived with a few thousand unarmed followers, he found the square empty and he and his attendants crowded in like surprised sightseers. A priest then appeared with a Bible to make a Christian of Atahualpa, but the Inca either dropped the book or threw it on the paving blocks. The Christians now had their excuse, to avenge dishonor to the Sacred Word, and opened fire. Some charged among the Indians on horseback, trampling down those they failed to fell with bullets. When they captured Atahualpa, his followers, like those of Huáscar earlier, considered themselves leaderless and deserted the cause. But two thousand to five thousand of them, depending on which account of the massacre you read, lay dead in the city square and streets.

Possibly Pizarro intended to free Huáscar if he agreed to be a puppet ruler. Perhaps Atahualpa only feared this would happen. In any case the Inca got word to men who remained loyal to him, and they reportedly drowned the half-brother before Pizarro's men gained control of Cuzco. Hoping to win his own freedom, Atahualpa promised to fill his prison room with riches as high as he could reach. Pizarro agreed and undoubtedly watched with delight as gold poured into the city. It came on the backs of llamas and the backs of men, with men carrying the heavier loads. Llamas refuse to move if given burdens of more than about forty pounds and spit at anyone who tries to overload them. The Spaniards feared Atahualpa and his influence too much to let him go. It is thought Almagro, who finally arrived with reinforcements, particularly objected to keeping the promise to free the Inca. The Spanish intended to burn the Indian leader at the stake, but when he agreed to let a priest baptize him, the Europeans provided a kinder death by strangling him. Pizarro now called the country New Castile, but most Spaniards

The Cathedral of Lima stands where Francisco Pizarro built the city's first church. At the left is the Archbishop's Palace

referred to it as Peru, possibly from the name of an Indian warrior they had conquered and admired.

Almagro and the Pizarros

Pizarro set about building a Spanish capital at Lima, a city he founded. Almagro fully expected to share in the land and gold, but Pizarro's half-brothers—Juan, Hernando, and Gonzalo—also demanded a generous share and tried to squeeze Almagro out. Pizarro now considered himself far superior to his former partner and sent Almagro off to quiet unrest in the north. Almagro had success along the coast, but inland he had to face forces led by Belalcázar, who had deserted the Pizarros and had gone to capture Quitu. Belalcázar had defeated the great Rumiñahui, local chieftain of the Quitu Indians who had taken control after Atahualpa and the Inca forces moved south. The conquistador claimed much of the north, called Quito by the Spanish. He refounded the capital, since the Indians had destroyed it to keep it from being of use to the white invaders, and named it Ville de San Francisco de Quito. Belalcázar made it obvious that Almagro could establish no domain for himself in that region. Passing back through Peru, Almagro tried his luck in Chile but was discouraged by the Mapuche Indians and the desolate Atacama Desert. His one hope seemed to be to force a place for himself in the highlands of Peru, where Indian uprisings gave the Pizarros trouble and had already caused Juan's death. With Indian help, Almagro captured Cuzco, which had been turned over to Hernando Pizarro. Possibly Almagro knew he couldn't hold out against the superior forces of Francisco Pizarro, or maybe he had little heart for resistance after years of struggle. He agreed to a truce and released the captive Hernando, though his years of association with Francisco should have warned him to expect trickery. When he met Hernando to negotiate, he walked into a trap. After holding Almagro prisoner a short while, Hernando ordered him strangled and, according to some reports, had his head chopped off as well.

While Hernando dealt with Almagro, Gonzalo Pizarro turned his attention to what the Spanish called Southern Peru, which became Bolivia. His arrival there in 1538 gave the Incas the strong leadership they had lacked during the six years since Atahualpa's betrayal. Many followed him willingly. Even the Aymara, who had successfully resisted being forced into the Inca empire, surrendered to the Spanish. Gonzalo's men soon made their way to the rich silver mines of the south central part of the country. Here they made their headquarters in an Indian village, Charcas, changing the name to La Plata and then to Chuquisaca. Gonzalo probably turned back before more than half of Southern Peru had been conquered, and in the same year he took over Quito, which Belalcázar had abandoned. Finding little gold in Quito, Belalcázar had moved north with his large army to seek the fabled land of El Dorado in what is now Colombia. With Belalcázar gone, the Pizarros feared "golden" Peru might be attacked by the Quitu Indians. To keep them subdued became Gonzalo's task.

In Search of Women Warriors

One of Gonzalo's best generals, Francisco de Orellana, thought he had see giant women warriors in one of his battles. When he had the opportunity, he wanted to search for these Amazons, as they were called

Fishermen on the Amazon River, which rises in the Peruvian Andes and flows across Brazil to the Atlantic. Called the "King of Waters," the Amazon is the largest river in the world since it carries more water than any other

after the women in Greek legend. With Quito firmly under their control, Gonzalo and Orellana took part of their army and headed east. In addition to Amazon women, they, like Belalcázar, hoped to find gold-rich El Dorado. After struging through dense jungle they came to a large river, most likely the Napo. Orellana set out to explore by boat while Gonzalo prepared for the return to Quito. When Orellana reached a larger river, he felt certain, because of its great width, that he was but a day or two from the ocean. No one realized the waterway covered nearly 4,000 miles. At times Orellana thought he saw the women warriors peering out from the tree-grown banks, but he probably saw Indian men wearing grass skirts. By the time he became aware of the great extent of the river, it was too late to turn back. Weeks later he reached the Atlantic, the first white man to travel a considerable portion of the waterway, and his tales of women warriors led to the river's being called the Amazon.

Days of Trouble

Gonzalo Pizarro waited and waited and waited for Orellana. Finally, in a fury, he broke camp and headed west. About two and a half years after leaving Quito, he returned with a handful of half-dead, half-naked survivors. He limped back into Quito to receive bad news concerning the other Pizarros. Hernando had been recalled to Spain to face charges of misconduct. Unable to justify his treatment of Almagro, he was imprisoned. Also, while Gonzalo was away, Francisco Pizarro had fared even worse. He and Hernando had taken from Almagro's followers whatever lands or other property they had possessed in Peru. These unfortunate men finally rallied behind Almagro's son, Diego Almagro, and stormed Francisco's palace. The men around Francisco Pizarro disliked him and now jumped out windows and slipped away through the gardens, leaving him to be stabbed to death. Gonzalo was the last of the Pizarros left in the New World.

Whatever his original intent, Diego Almagro found himself in control of the government. Barely out of his teens, he tried to hold off the armies of Spain and make Peru his own kingdom. This threw the country into a civil war, and within a year Almagro met defeat and was beheaded. Cristobal Vaca de Castro led the forces for Charles I of Spain, and he became governor of the colony. One of his main chores was to replace the Pizarro system in Peru with the "New Laws of 1542" designed to improve life for the Indians. The Pizarros had granted land generously to their captains, and the Indians on the land went to the new owners as laborers, really as slaves. Under this encomienda system the native peoples received such harsh treatment that the Catholic priests, who had permitted much in the way of cruelty during the conquest, complained. The "New Laws" promised the Indians a degree of emancipation, but the old soldiers who now held hundreds of square miles refused to change and civil war continued. Vaca de Castro fled back to Spain while Gonzalo Pizarro came south from Quito to champion the cause of the landholders. Within a short time Peru fell under his leadership, and for a few years he was "king" of a domain stretching from Panama to Chile and Argentina. The King of Spain sent Father Pedro de la Gasca to put down the rebellion. This able diplomat withdrew the "New Laws," thereby destroying part of Gonzalo's cause, and pardoned many of Gonzalo's followers. By the time the priest's soldiers faced Gonzalo in battle, the last of the Pizarros in Peru had a weak and unreliable force. Seeing they would be defeated, some of Gonzalo's men changed sides; he was trying to hack these traitors down when finally taken prisoner. Father la Gasca found Gonzalo guilty of treason and ordered him beheaded the next day.

During the period of unrest, Peru had been made a viceroyalty—a region ruled by a viceroy who answered to the king appointing him. Included within its boundaries were most sections of South America except Venezuela and Brazil. Such a huge area could hardly be governed well from Lima, so Spain introduced the *audiencia* system. Under this, various parts of the viceroyalty had a measure of self-government, especially when it came to hearing, or holding an audience of, their own legal disputes. Quito became the seat of an *audiencia* in 1563 and led a relatively peaceful existence for two hundred and fifty years. Because coastal Indians made reluctant slaves, Negroes were brought to the port towns, where they became a significant part of the population.

Tin ore comes down to a processing plant from Potosí's "rich hill" by buckets on an endless cable

Alto Peru

The Southern Peru of Gonzalo Pizarro took the official name of Alto (Upper) Peru. About 1545 the "rich hill" in the south proved to be the greatest silver discovery of the region, and Potosí was founded. This settlement grew rapidly until, with a population of nearly 200,000, it became South America's largest city. In 1559 Chuquisaca was made the seat of an *audiencia*. As Chuquisaca and Potosí lay a great distance from Lima over rough terrain, the Spanish founded La Paz as an important way station. La Paz developed into a center of discontent, and one of the first rebellions against the Viceroyalty of Peru occurred here. During the second half of the 1600s and throughout the 1700s uprisings continued to take place in Alto Peru. Always they involved the Criollos—pure-blooded Spaniards born in the New World—and some mestizos, or people of Spanish and Indian blood. These men hated the *audiencia* system that put most important governmental posts into the hands of men sent from Spain. As trouble increased in every region of Spanish South America, Charles III took some territory from Peru's control in 1776 to establish the Viceroyalty of La Plata. Alto Peru came under this new division, but now it had to answer to Buenos Aires, Argentina, instead of Lima and so was even farther from the center of government. This hardly brought peace.

Changes for the Indians

As trouble brewed among the Criollos and mestizos of the various colonies, the Indian populations grew more peaceful. Tupac Amaru, the last direct descendant of Manco Capac, started an uprising in 1565, but after seven years of raids on Spanish settlements, he was captured and killed. He fell to the forces of Francisco de Toledo, one of the early and one of the few efficient viceroys of Peru. Toledo demanded improved conditions for Indians forced to work in mines, but officials mostly ignored him, and viceroys following him gave little thought to the native peoples. More than two hundred years after Tupac Amaru's death, his mestizo descendant José Gabriel Condorcanqui (Tupac Amaru II) led an equally unsuccessful revolt, though it did win a few improvements for the Indian peoples.

In general, the Indians turned from warfare to stealing. Under the Incas theft had been a serious crime, but when the Indians saw that looting was commonplace with the conquistadors, they gradually accepted stealing as a way of life. Otherwise they adopted Spanish ways slowly, though in agriculture they found the white men could offer

A sturdy little burro will carry much heavier loads than a temperamental llama

The market at Laja, near La Paz, is spread out before the village church, now more than three hundred years old. This site on the altiplano almost became the Spanish headquarters between Sucre and Cuzco, Peru, but lack of protection from cold winds drove the people to settle where La Paz now stands

several improvements. Domesticated pigs and sheep made better eating than llamas, while horses and burros provided animals the Indians could ride. It was always the man who rode, and still today the Indian woman follows behind on foot. Both the Spaniards and Indians soon learned that horses belonged in the lowlands, not on the altiplano. Horses cannot get enough oxygen in the high altitude and much hard work or running kills them. The Incas had turned the soil with pointed sticks. The Spaniards introduced a plow pulled by oxen or burros, and this the Indians adopted. The Spaniards planted barley, alfalfa, wheat, and various types of green beans. They brought peaches from Spain, cherries from Mexico, and also introduced plums, pears, apples, and apricots. By the early years of the 1600s the land had been turned over to Indian families to work but not to own. They had escaped slavery, but much of what they produced went to the Spanish landowners.

In the heart of Lima, Peru, Plaza San Martín with its monument to the great liberator from Argentina

Changes for Everybody

By the 1700s South America had ceased to produce shiploads of treasure for Spain, and what was produced sometimes fell into the hands of English and French pirates. As a result, greedy officials in Madrid claimed the encomiendas. Without coming to the New World to manage their lands themselves they gained little, for the old owners stayed on as overseers and robbed the absent landholders at every opportunity. To get some return, the men in Spain sold the land back to private individuals or gave it to officials as rewards. As the encomiendas were parceled out, they were replaced by haciendas (smaller acreages), and these still prevail in much of South America today.

A university, founded in Chuquisaca in 1624, became a center of discontent, and in May, 1809, its teachers promoted a rebellion. Peru and Quito also had uprisings later that year, but all ended in disaster for the rebels. Leaders received brief trials and quick deaths, but they inspired a generation of followers. It was not by accident that many revolts occurred at this time. In Europe Napoleon Bonaparte had crowned himself emperor of France in 1804. After forcing Charles IV of Spain to abdicate in 1808, Napoleon put his oldest brother, Joseph Bonaparte, on the Spanish throne. Restless men in the New World, already unhappy at being treated as inferior to judges sent out from Spain, cared even less for being subordinate to officials picked by a Frenchman. As they recalled the revolt of the thirteen American colonies from England in 1776 and of Haiti from France in 1804, a few of them dreamed of independence from Spain. Probably more hoped for provincial status, under which they would enjoy internal self-government while still recognizing the king of Spain as their monarch. The savage brutality of the royalist forces in putting down the early revolts caused many men to think of complete independence.

San Martín, Bolívar, and Sucre

The first successful revolts in South America took place outside the central Andes. José de San Martín of Argentina received a military education in Spain and became an officer there at the age of fifteen. Napoleon's invasion of Portugal and Spain gave him experience in leading troops, which he used in the cause of liberty as soon as he returned home in 1812. The movement for Argentine independence had already started, but taking command of the rebel forces, he kept the Spanish from recapturing lost ground. After Argentina's independence had been declared in 1816, he prepared to invade Chile. Once Chile had its freedom, he turned his attention to Peru, knowing no South American countries were safe from reconquest until the viceroyalty in Lima had been destroyed. He hired Thomas Cochrane, a disgraced British naval officer, and collected a mismatched assortment of vessels. Cochrane landed him on Peruvian soil in 1820 and protected his flank by driving off Spanish reinforcements that came by sea. San Martín marched toward Lima, defeating one after another of the royalist groups sent against him until at last Spanish officials agreed to negotiate with him.

The Spaniards failed to offer self-government for Peru, so San Martín marched on. Not until Lima lay within his grasp did he halt his army. He didn't want Peruvians saying he had forced independence on them against their will. But when they invited him to enter Lima he did so, to proclaim the country's independence on July 28, 1821.

Simón Bolívar, during several years of gay living in Europe, gradually became concerned with liberty for South America. His first target was his homeland, Venezuela. After initial successes followed by setbacks and exile, he finally assured his country's freedom in June 1821, by defeating royalist forces in the north central state of Carabobo. In the process of liberating Venezuela, he gained independence for Colombia and then combined the two countries as one—Gran Colombia. With Peruvian independence a month later, Quito lay between two free regions. It was in a state of rebellion, with the city of Guayaquil having

The monument to Simón Bolívar reminds the people of La Paz of their country's struggle for independence

withdrawn from the capital's control in 1820. Although Bolívar received no invitation to come to Guayaquil's aid, his ambition led him to enter the colony of Quito. One of his finest generals was Antonio José de Sucre, also a Venezuelan by birth. Sucre sailed to Guayaquil, quieted disturbances there, and then marched toward the capital, to be faced on the slopes of Mt. Pichincha by soldiers loyal to Spain. With the aid of Peruvian rebels sent by San Martín, Sucre won a decisive victory on May 24, 1822, and assured the colony's independence. It took the name Republic of Ecuador, since it lay across the equator, and Bolívar made it part of Gran Colombia.

San Martín failed to win popularity in Peru. Completely honest by nature, he refused bribes and gave no favors to the aristocrats. After Bolívar's forces occupied Ecuador, San Martín went to Guayaquil to meet with the Venezuelan liberator. No record was made of the discussions held between these two great leaders, so opposite from one another. It is thought that fun-loving, flamboyant Bolívar offered his services to quiet, serious San Martín, and that San Martín, suspecting his followers would object to this, refused the offer. Perhaps because of his poor health, San Martín agreed to withdraw from northwestern South America altogether. In any case, San Martín went home to Argentina while Bolívar occupied Lima and put down the unrest that threatened Peruvian independence. With relative peace obtained in Ecuador and the Peruvian lowlands, Bolívar sent Sucre to the aid of rebel groups in the mountains. Again Sucre proved to be a brilliant leader. While still in Peru, he defeated royalists in two major battles, with his greatest victory coming on December 9, 1824, when he captured the Spanish Viceroy, José de la Serna. Then he marched into Alto Peru, where the city of Chuquisaca changed its name to Sucre to honor him. As no word came from Bolívar as to the course he should follow, Sucre declared Alto Peru's independence in La Paz on February 9, 1825. The new country paid tribute to Bolívar by taking the name Bolivia. Now all three countries of the central Andes were free and ready to go more or less separate ways.

Modern Peru

Shortly before his death in 1830, Simón Bolívar reportedly wailed, "America is ungovernable." He spoke from frustration, perhaps because he had failed to become dictator of all South America, but history shows he was close to the truth. No South American willingly surrenders his authority to a central government. Bolívar had probably intended to include Peru and Bolivia in Gran Colombia, but Sucre set up a separate government in Bolivia and unrest warned Bolívar against such a move in Peru. Before long uprisings in the north called Bolívar to Colombia, and he withdrew from Peru even though he had been named president-for-life of that country. General José de La Mar (Lamar) became Peru's new president. Once he had asked Bolívar to make himself emperor of Peru, but now he tore up Bolívar's constitution and attempted to make sure the Venezuelan liberator would have no chance to return. He encouraged malcontents in Bolivia to unseat Sucre. This caused Bolívar to send an army across Ecuador toward Peru, which La Mar went to meet. Forced out of Bolivia by Andrés Santa Cruz, Sucre sailed to Ecuador, took charge of the army against La Mar, and defeated him. Peru found itself in need of another leader before it had become used to the last one. This proved to be a trend.

General Agustín Gamarra took the reins of government with a stranglehold. The National Convention, or Congress, tried to replace him with General Luis José Orbegoso, but Gamarra's army chased Orbegoso and the Convention out of Lima. Failing to receive the rewards they wanted for their action, the soldiers soon changed sides,

Cities of the central Andes retain a Spanish touch in being built around central squares. Frequently, as in Arequipa, Peru, the central square is dominated by the Cathedral

In the name of progress and modernity, many communities of the central Andes have lost most of their Spanish heritage, but Arequipa, Peru, keeps some interesting arcaded walks around the central plaza

and Gamarra fled to Cuzco. Orbegoso sent Felipe Santiago de Salaverry to capture Gamarra. A revolt in Arequipa drew Orbegoso to southern Peru, and while he was away Salaverry returned to Lima and proclaimed himself president. And so it went. Gamarra routed Orbegoso from southern Peru, Orbegoso sought aid from Bolivian dictator Andrés Santa Cruz, Santa Cruz chased Gamarra out of Cuzco, Gamarra took over Arequipa, Salaverry rushed south to recapture Arequipa, William Miller of Santa Cruz's army captured Salaverry, and Santa Cruz declared Peru, Bolivia, and Ecuador united in a federation.

From Federation to Civil War

The federation had a short life. Santa Cruz had Salaverry shot, a pointless, unpopular move that caused riots in southern Peru. Chile had probably been eyeing that section of Peru for some time, as it included the northern part of the nitrate-rich Atacama Desert. With the excuse that the unrest threatened her freedom and commerce, Chile declared war on Santa Cruz's federation. Argentina backed Chile. Peruvian ships in southern waters fell to Chilean commanders. Then Chilean troops landed north of Lima and pushed toward the capital. Santa Cruz received little support in Lima, where his tyranny had made him unpopular, and he retreated into the Andes. When he finally made a stand, the Chileans defeated him, bringing to an end his federation of three years. He sailed for Europe and left Peru to its game of "dictatorial fruit basket upset."

Gamarra, with Chilean backing, regained control of the government. No man in Peru at that time was more hated. His final mistake was to try to bring Bolivia and Peru again under one government, for which purpose he invaded Bolivia. After he met defeat and death about halfway between the border and La Paz, Peru degenerated into a pack of warring cities. It took General Manuel Agostín Vivanco and his wife, each leading a separate army, to quiet the civil war in the central and southern regions, but they failed to unite Peru. One of Sucre's able generals now gained national prominence by defeating Vivanco and ending the civil war. This mestizo, Ramón Castilla, had fought against San Martín as a teen-ager but had changed sides as he matured. Now he proved to be the caudillo, or strong man, of which Peru had a desperate need.

Caudillo Rule

After he won the presidency in 1845, Castilla freed the Negro slaves and promoted better treatment for the Indians. He launched a program of railroad building and had distant regions of the country linked by telegraph. Instead of falling to some military coup, he retired at the end of his term and chose a successor for the presidency. That successor hoped to be more than a puppet, so Castilla ousted him after four years. Confirmed in office by the Congress the following year, Castilla eventually gave Peru a new constitution, the fourth it had had in thirty-two years. This one remained in force well into the twentieth century. As caudillo, Castilla cut down military expenditures while increasing school-building programs. For a time he reduced a few of the heavy taxes on the Indians. He could do this because of guano. Even before he came to power, officials discovered that Europeans would pay good money for guano to be used as fertilizer. Castilla exported it recklessly. While Peruvian soil grew poorer, the deposits of dung on the nearby islands were shoveled or blasted loose to bring wealth into the treasury. The government controlled a monopoly on the guano export, but a few men chosen to handle trade in this commodity grew extremely rich.

At the end of his six-year term Castilla again retired peacefully, but this time he could not dictate his country's course from behind the scenes. For all his reforms, he had done far more for men who didn't need help than for the poor mestizos and Indians. The schools he built served the wealthy, as did the railroads and telegraph lines. Yet without the nearly two decades of peace he brought to Peru it seems possible that no worthwhile advances would have been made at all. Few occurred in the two decades following his retirement in 1862.

For forty years Spain had watched South America for an opportunity to recapture her lost colonies. The unrest that followed Castilla's retirement gave the mother country courage. In 1865 she landed troops on the Chincha Islands as the first step toward invading the continent anew. But in the following year she bungled. Spanish ships shelled Valparaiso, Chile's main port, and brought sudden and unexpected cooperation between Chile and Peru. Ecuador and Bolivia came to the aid of their neighbors, and Spain's attempt to capture the port city of Callao met with defeat. Thirteen years of negotiating and stalling followed, but in 1879 Spain finally recognized Peru as an independent country.

A Railroad to the Sky

With Castilla out of power, there remained no great generals from the wars of independence to lead Peru. The presidents who followed him put their personal interests ahead of national ones. When José Balta

The famous old fort of Callao, now a major Peruvian military headquarters, still stands near the waterfront

came to power, his personal interest seemed to be to build a monument to himself. Not just a statue on a pedestal would do. He wanted something uniquely magnificent to stand for all time as a tribute to his leadership. What could do it better than a railroad over the Andes, a trackway to the stars that several sober engineers said couldn't be built? Henry Meiggs, who had barely escaped the police of San Francisco, California, because of forgery charges, was building railroads in Chile. Unaware of Meiggs' past, Balta contracted with him for the line over the Andes that carried the country to ruin. As it passed through a tunnel 15,700 feet above sea level, this railroad became the highest standard-gauge line in the world. But its cost went up faster than its tracks. The president borrowed money from European nations for the railroad and for harbor improvements and other public works, but in time the interest on the loans each year amounted to more than came into the country. Peru was bankrupt.

Meiggs also had trouble. In the valleys his road followed, the laborers contracted verruga, a bacterial disease carried by sandflies. Suddenly a man developed a headache, he vomited or had diarrhea, and his temperature shot up. Soon painful lumps appeared on his head and legs, while he grew weak from anemia. Laborers deserted in order to escape the disease. Meiggs brought coolies from China, telling them nothing of Peruvian verruga you can be sure. But they couldn't stand hard work at high altitudes. Mountain fever, from insufficient oxygen, brought on nausea and headaches until they collapsed and had to be carried to the lowlands. Pouring his newly acquired riches into the railroad in a frantic effort to complete it, Meiggs too ran out of money. Some Peruvians like to tell romantic tales of how he collapsed and died beside his line, as penniless as when he had fled San Francisco. Actually, he completed the road and spent his last years in near poverty in Lima, getting an occasional job to plan a park or some other public improvement.

Civilian Rule

Balta was assassinated by a family of his relatives whom he had double-crossed, and Manuel Pardo came to power. For the first time, Peru had a civilian rather than a military leader, and part of Pardo's program was to reduce the influence of the army. He cut spending, thereby angering everyone who had been making money from Balta's lavish building programs. In place of encouraging extravagance and waste, he fostered education, cultural activities, and taxes against men who could afford to pay as well as against men who couldn't. Many historians outside Peru think he may have been the greatest leader the country ever had. He completed his four-year term (the period had been changed by Castilla's new constitution) and entered the Senate. There he fought so openly against allowing increased powers to army officers that he had to run for his life. On his return from exile, he became president of the Senate. Again he opposed the military, and this time an army assassin ended his life.

More War

With Pardo's death, military leaders took firm control and rushed the country toward a new disaster. At this time Peru claimed the northern part of the Atacama Desert, along with the coastal cities Arica and Iqueque. Bolivia held the central part of the desert area and another valuable port, Antofagasta. Although Peru had become increasingly active in mining the nitrate deposits of the north, Bolivia had done little. Chileans had worked their way into the desert and many mines were operated almost entirely by them except for British technicians and officials. Bolivia benefited by placing duties on minerals taken from her territory or exported through Antofagasta. Foreseeing that these duties could eat up her profits, Chile asked Bolivia to sign an agreement not to increase the taxes. Bolivia soon regretted signing and broke the agreement. She moved to take over Chilean mines, as Peru had already taken over some of the mines farther north. When Chile's troops quickly occupied Antofagasta, Bolivia declared war. Peru held back even though she had a secret mutual-defense treaty with Bolivia, but since she wouldn't yield to certain Chilean demands, Chile declared war on her. The costly "fertilizer war," more properly known as the War of the Pacific, was on.

Few reports on what occurred during the war agree with one another. Peruvians and Bolivians claim the Chileans acted with prehistoric savagery, butchering civilians as well as soldiers and firing on undefended areas. Chileans say all areas were defended and Peruvians made it necessary for them to invade residential sections of leading cities to seek troops hiding there. Peruvians charge that Chileans looted and burned every store in sight, while the Chileans answer by saying the Peruvian populace itself did the looting and burning. Without question, Peru suffered terribly. Her ships soon rested on the bottom of the sea, while almost every industrial plant within shelling distance of the coast lay in ruins. Business came to a standstill. As the war dragged on for four years, the army called on both older and younger men until nearly every male between sixteen and sixty from the more populous areas had a taste of battle. So many were killed that the country lacked young, energetic men to rebuild Peru after fighting ceased.

A half dozen governments tried to manage Peruvian affairs during the war and the negotiations immediately following. Finally one was assembled that agreed to Chilean terms, after which the conquering forces withdrew from devastated Lima. The city has been rebuilt, but the Chileans left a hatred that has not entirely disappeared to this day. The conquerors continued to occupy Peru's southern cities of Tacna and Arica while bargaining went on for nearly fifty years. In 1929 the United States helped arrange a treaty that put Tacna back in Peruvian hands but left Arica and everything south of there to Chile. By taking part in the negotiations, the United States did herself no good in the eyes of Peruvians. North American mining interests had replaced many of the British ones in the desert area over which the war was fought, so her role in seeking a treaty inevitably looked selfish, even greedy, to people in Peru.

Saving the Country

After the "fertilizer war" ended in 1883, Peru faced the prospect of being divided among the nations from which she had borrowed money to fight. But foreign investors in the United States and Britain agreed to take over her debts in exchange for generous concessions. This put Peru's external trade and much of her internal commerce into the hands of outsiders, but it did give the country a chance to recuperate. At this time two Peruvian strong men emerged. One was Andrés Cáceres, the only general never defeated by the Chileans. When it became obvious that he intended to dictate from the president's chair or from behind the scenes, he faced an army of discontented Peruvians and lost. Nicolás de Píerola took charge. With a love of spectacle that appealed to Peruvians, he gained wide popularity, though he accomplished no more than Cáceres. The main thing these two men did was give the country a period of relative peace in which to offset the devastation of war.

Except for mining, Peru has never had much in the way of heavy industry. The country depends more on small factories and the products of her fields. Particularly after the War of the Pacific, agriculture helped rescue the country. Cotton became a major export and so did sugar. Small factories to turn the cotton fiber into cloth or finished garments developed. At the time Peru was recovering, scientists were experimenting with drugs to relieve pain and make surgery more practical. They discovered that cocaine, made from coca leaves, served as a powerful anesthetic, and a cocaine industry emerged in Peru. Mining companies were eager to explore the Andes in search of mineral sources. They already knew that quantities of copper existed in the mountains and soon made new discoveries. Today more than a dozen minerals

Laborers carry huge and heavy loads in the central Andes. This man is almost hidden by a large bale of jute that he is bringing from the Amazon River to a warehouse in Iquitos

The well-to-do people of the central Andes have modern homes and well-kept lawns just as people of North America and Europe do

figure among the country's exports. Oil was found in the north about the time the War of the Pacific started, and after the war a petroleum industry grew up along the coast.

With the coming of World War I, Peru's products found a steady market and the country, though not rich, escaped extreme poverty. Yet hardly an Indian had reason to be aware of this. Although only the Indians could survive the hard work in the mines, they received the least amount of benefit from the work they did. Wealthy Peruvians grew richer and foreign investors profited greatly, but the men who really kept the mines producing lived in crowded huts, ate less than one good meal a day, and chewed coca leaves to anesthetize their stomachs against hunger pains. When the coca inevitably affected their health and made it impossible for them to work, they lost their jobs and faced charity from their relatives or starvation.

A New Breed of Warriors

Presidents came and went without making much impression. They all belonged to the wealthy class (and still do today). In politics, Peru appeared to be without a conscience. But among her intellectuals a few

The presidential palace in Lima looks old, but most of it was reconstructed between 1939 and 1942

men refused to be blinded by returning prosperity. Surprisingly enough, the most outspoken critic came from the aristocracy. Manuel González Prada had the wealth and leisure to devote himself to writing. He became a poet with a difference. Growing up during the period of romantic writers in South America, González Prada saw his world realistically. Everywhere he looked he observed graft, prejudice, exploitation. Instead of supporting the men of his class, he attacked them for their treatment of the Indians. He called on the Indians to revolt. Indians who could read Spanish passed his words along to the millions who couldn't. They looked to him as to a savior, yet did almost nothing to practice what he preached. His words stirred more activity among Peru's slowly developing middle class.

José Carlos Mariátegui went beyond González Prada. He not only advocated revolt but hoped to lead the rebels into a Marxist state. González Prada had many revolutionary ideas, but he was not a Communist. Mariátegui was. Following Mariátegui, the student Victor Raúl

Haya de la Torre came on the scene. He founded a party, the *Alianza Popular Revolucionaria Americana,* and carried it well beyond Peru's borders. In this he may partly have defeated his own purpose. When candidates of the APRA have won a presidential election in Peru, they have been refused a chance to take control on the grounds that the party is international rather than Peruvian. When Haya himself ran for the presidency the first time, he supposedly lost through fraud. A mass of people stood behind him ready to put him in office by force, but he poured soft words on their wrath. Many men in Peru believe in APRA's original goals of help for the Indians and poor mestizos, putting all local industries in Peruvian hands, ridding the country of foreign investments, and making the Panama Canal an international waterway. One goal however, forming a United States of South America, has fewer supporters.

Reforms and Dictators

While González Prada and his disciples failed to bring about a revolution, they forced more than one president to introduce changes. José Pardo, elected for the first time in 1904 and again during World War I, was unusually liberal for Peru. He passed legislation for compulsory

The palace guards are colorfully dressed in uniforms much like those the Europeans wore during the eighteenth and nineteenth centuries

79

education and built schools. He started sanitation and other health programs, and arranged for improved treatment of Indian workers on haciendas. In time he was able to reduce labor for women and children, but it took a nearly nationwide strike at the end of World War I before he did much to cut down the laboring hours of able-bodied men. Augusto Bernardino Leguía served as minister of finance during Pardo's first term and as president between Pardo's terms. Though he probably had won the election of 1918, Leguía seized power immediately just to make sure. In his second period as president, he quickly established himself as dictator. He replaced Castilla's constitution of 1860 with one of his own which would permit him to succeed himself. He suppressed freedom of the press and closed Lima's university for three years. Once having been a *Civilista*—the party opposed to military rule —he now appeared to be a party unto himself. The people he had promised to aid, the Indians, received no more help than they had before, while the wealthy class grew wealthier. If the middle class grew larger, it was accidentally due to the overflow of benefits from the aristocracy. To Leguía, the United States represented progress, so he lavishly handed out concessions to North American firms. The navy and the educational system were turned over to Americans to be improved. British and other foreign interests suffered as a consequence, while anti-American hatred increased among Peruvian students and people with a strong national point of view.

Nationalists accused Leguía of giving away parts of the country as well as its minerals and other products. It was during his eleven years in office that Chile received Arica. Colombia took a large strip between the Putumayo and Amazon rivers, giving it the valuable Amazonian port of Leticia. And huge estates turned over to members of the Leguía family kept hundreds of thousands of acres out of the hands of the poor people who needed them. Even so, with sewers for major cities, health programs, irrigation projects, improved roads, more railroads, and other public works, Leguía might have remained in office if it had not been for a worldwide depression. As international business fell off at the close of the 1920s, he could not pay interest on the national debt he had accumulated. Haya de la Torre and his APRA party were stirring up the common man, while army officers like Luis Sánchez Cerro, a wealthy mestizo, were rousing the military. A revolt of the people in Arequipa frightened the upper class into acting before the lower classes could snatch the government from their control, and in 1930 Colonel Sánchez Cerro overthrew Leguía. Sánchez Cerro was followed by other caudillos.

Changing Times

At times, to weaken the APRA party, the presidents of Peru have accepted help from Communist organizations. In protest, APRA has swung from left of center toward the right. For a few years in the mid-1940s, a rightist president received support from Haya. But the military threw him out at the first opportunity and Haya sought asylum in the embassy of Colombia. Peruvian soldiers dug trenches around the building and prepared to shoot him if he so much as showed himself at a window. He lived in the embassy for six years before he was allowed to go into exile in Mexico. Though he celebrated his seventy-third birthday in 1968, some labor unionists still hope he will lead them to power someday. Many students and Indians, however, are looking to other parties.

The strongest new party of recent times has been the *Acción Popular* of Fernando Belaúnde Terry. Belaúnde, after an education in the United States, entered Peruvian politics in his early thirties. He made a name for himself with housing programs for the middle class, which made the lower classes hope he would do something for them as well. To assure them he would, he campaigned in the villages and rural areas of Peru, something presidential aspirants had never done before. He won the presidency in 1963, partly because of promises to provide land for the needy Indians. The Communists and certain other groups are crying for just such a program, yet Belaúnde made little progress because the Congress was divided among too many parties besides his own. Even parties that had the same aims as his blocked his efforts because they wanted the credit for reforms and would not let him have it.

At the start of Belaúnde's term, Peru showed friendship for the United States. The country prospered, and as long as its affairs went

A fisherman of Chucuito, Peru, repairs his nets. Chucuito is part of the western suburbs of Callao and its population is of Italian descent

well it remained friendly. But when Peru ran into trouble, its feeling for the States rapidly cooled. In 1966 more than one-fourth of Peru's export revenue came from the sale of fish meal, used in livestock feed. Substitutes for this product came on the market and made the price drop. Manufacturers of fish meal faced having to sell for a loss, so they began to store their product in hopes of waiting until the price went up once more. This meant no export duties, and Belaúnde's government found itself short of funds. Although the United States offered loans to help out during the emergency, it requested the Peruvian government to cut down on careless spending to keep the loans from being frittered away. Belaúnde refused the loans on those terms. Among the things for which Peru was spending money were jet fighter planes. When the United States interfered with her getting them from Great Britain, Peru ordered them from France. Belaúnde said the country needed them to offset the threat of Communist guerrillas based in Chile, but outside observers felt this was not the whole picture. Whatever the truth, guerrilla raids increased in the late 1960s. The raiders expected aid from the unhappy Indians, but they got support, in words more often than in serious actions, from university students. Regardless of the reason for the planes, there was a danger that Peru would set off a Latin American arms race. After Belaúnde was ousted in 1968, the Peruvian government still sought to build up its fighting power.

Every president of Peru has to make certain choices. On the local scene he must decide whether or not to call on the legislature to enact laws that will benefit the common man. If he does so, he will anger men of his own class, for all of Peru's presidents come from well-to-do families. In general these families believe that aiding one group cuts the foundation out from under another. Since Congress consists of men from these families, a president who opposes them may lose power, prestige, and the presidency without ever getting a liberal bill passed. At the same time he should make some pretense of doing something, for probably he will have campaigned on a platform calling for change. If the masses get restless over his inactivity, they too can bring about his downfall. On an international level a president faces a choice between isolationism and being accused of giving away the country's resources. He must be especially careful in his dealings with the United States whenever anti-American feelings are strong in his country. Yet trying to cut Peru off completely from United States financial and technical aid may leave the country and its industries without the money or the know-how needed to keep up-to-date. And any country that wants to prosper today must stay abreast of the times. Peruvians know this, and so every president who comes to power will try to be a juggler and keep everybody contented.

Bolivia Up-to-Date

After General Sucre defeated the Spanish royalists at Ayacucho, which is in Peru rather than Bolivia, he waited for word from Bolívar as to his next move. No one knows why his commander failed to respond. Sucre marched on to La Paz, where he announced the country's independence on February 9, 1825. He called together an assembly to plan the country's future, and it has been said he suggested naming the country in honor of Bolívar to appease the Liberator in case he was displeased with the steps Sucre had taken. This could well be a myth, but the country did call itself the Republic of Bolívar briefly and then Bolivia. Sucre's Decree of Independence brought Bolívar out of his silence. He said Sucre had no right to decide the region's course without consulting leaders in other countries, particularly Peru and Argentina since Bolivia had been most closely linked with them in colonial days. But Sucre stood by his acts. In doing so he opposed not only Bolívar but also the officer who was his second in command of the army occupying Bolivia.

Bolívar probably wanted Peru and Bolivia joined as one country, which would have made him president of the entire region. Sucre's second in command, Andrés Santa Cruz, definitely wanted the two countries to be united, along with Ecuador, as they had been in Inca times. Disregarding their wishes, the assembly that met voted for independence. Bolívar refused to recognize their authority, but when a Peruvian Congress assembled a year later and accepted the Bolivian decision, Bolívar had no further argument against it. Besides, the Bolivian Congress chose him to be the first president of the new coun-

An arch on a mountain ridge in La Paz reminds people of the successful Bolivian revolution of 1952. Seen through it is Illimani, 21,184 feet high, and one of the most famous Andean peaks in the country

try. As president of both Peru and Bolivia and as the formulator of constitutions for both lands, he may have felt he was uniting them. He had reason to get over this feeling in a hurry. The countries lacked internal let alone external unity, and he could not keep Peru peaceful while he occupied himself with affairs in Bolivia. After being president of Bolivia a little more than a year, he handed the presidency to Sucre and hastened back to Lima.

Sucre and Santa Cruz

At this time, Sucre stood next to Bolívar as the leading hero of Bolivia. Once he declared the country's independence and called for an assembly to plan its course, he had returned to his military duties. He pursued the last of the royalist forces, led by Pedro Antonio de Olañeta, and defeated them in April, 1825. With this last major battle he ended Spain's military strength on the continent. He also reached the peak of his popularity. While he was a soldier fighting for their benefit,

Bolivians loved him. Once Bolívar put control of the government in Sucre's hands, the local people saw him as a different man. Had he been given a choice, Sucre would have let somebody else be president, but he found himself in charge and did the best he could. Affairs went badly. Bolívar's constitution gave him insufficient power to dictate the country's course. Unlike men who followed him, he respected constitutions and tried to abide by them. Aware of the restlessness of the country, he kept his army standing by. This only made Bolivians more restless, for many of the soldiers came from Bolívar's Gran Colombia— Venezuela, Colombia, Ecuador. Local Criollos now saw Sucre as the leader of an army of occupation rather than as a liberator.

Santa Cruz, a mestizo, particularly disliked having his country in foreign hands. His Indian mother supposedly traced her ancestry back to Inca royalty, and he probably thought of himself as an Indian prince. This accounts for his ambition to bring the lands of the Inca empire back together as one nation. For a short while it looked as if he might be successful. After withdrawing from Bolivia, Bolívar made Santa Cruz second in power to Sucre. Before long Bolívar called Santa Cruz to Lima to be president of the council of government there. When Bolívar found it necessary to leave in order to hold Gran Colombia together, Santa Cruz became acting president of Peru. His chance seemed to be approaching, but Peruvians looked on him in the same way he looked on Sucre in La Paz. He was an outsider. Had he realized the feeling against him, he might have seized power instead of taking a chance on losing out in an election. General La Mar defeated him and Santa Cruz sadly returned to his own country.

Once back in La Paz, he worked vigorously for the overthrow of Sucre, encouraged by La Mar in Peru and many Bolivian Criollos. At last he was rewarded, for Sucre withdrew in 1828, aware that as matters stood he could be of little use to the country. Santa Cruz worked quickly to be put in Sucre's place, after which he established himself as dictator. As La Mar had done in Peru, he replaced Bolívar's constitution. Any uprising within the nation's borders quickly felt the force of his army, though no one was exactly sure where the borders lay. Roughly, the country occupied 900,000 square miles between the

Pacific Ocean and the Paraguay River. It was a land of empty spaces, for only the altiplano had many inhabitants.

With Bolivia firmly in his hands, Santa Cruz again thought of bringing his country and Peru together. He drew up a treaty of trade between the two countries as one step toward uniting them. In the mid-1830s unrest in Peru gave him the chance he wanted. Luis José Orbegoso, chosen president of Peru by the National Convention but unable to take office because Agustín Gamarra stood in his way, asked Santa Cruz for help. Santa Cruz's forces sent Gamarra into hiding and captured another claimant to the Peruvian presidency, Santiago de Salaverry. The Bolivian dictator promptly declared Peru and Bolivia united in a federation, which was also supposed to include Ecuador though he had little chance to enforce his claim on that country. Orbegoso became "president" of one section of Peru. Chile and Argentina were too alarmed at the sudden emergence of a large nation in the north to stand idly by and let it gain strength. Besides, Chile had an interest in the nitrate mines of the Atacama Desert, which might be closed to her if a powerful Peru-Bolivia developed. With Argentine support, Chile attacked Santa Cruz's federation and in three years broke it apart. Santa Cruz retreated into exile, his dream of a reborn Inca empire shattered, and Orbegoso also had to flee. Bolivia became a battleground for military officers seeking power and glory and more often finding frustration or death. None of them could equal Santa Cruz, who is sometimes called the most outstanding native-born leader Bolivia has ever had.

Terrorism Follows Santa Cruz

While Peru fortunately acquired a dictator, Castilla, who provided a period of peace in which the country could develop, Bolivia had an era of slaughter. Commerce had little chance to grow. If a man with a business or factory backed a new leader one day, he might find his leader dead and his property burned the next. Personal rights and possessions amounted to very little where every man's goal seemed to be to reach the top by whatever means possible. Only the Indians went quietly about their business of trying to scrape a living from the soil. Even a final threat to Bolivia's independence failed to bring harmony

88

Bolivian Indians have always had a difficult life on the altiplanos. In hopes of an improved future, however, these highland women help to clear a site for a community center and workshop

within the country. Perhaps if a real war or one of any duration had developed, the picture would have changed. But when President Gamarra of Peru marched across the border and toward La Paz, General José Ballivián went out to meet him and defeated him quickly. This made Ballivián enough of a hero that he briefly held the presidency, but after a year and a half in control he slipped away into exile to save his skin.

As far as anyone knows, elections invariably lacked honesty. A man had to be able to read and write and had to own property to vote, which excluded most Indians and a great many mestizos. But even if the lower classes could have had a voice at the ballot box, the results would probably have been the same. The military controlled the country, and an officer occupied the presidency only because of the strength of his soldiers. In the late 1840s it momentarily looked as if a spokesman for the lower classes had appeared. Manuel Isidoro Belzú promised the poor people he would come to their aid and wooed them to support him, even though they couldn't vote. He gained control of the government through a military rather than a popular revolt and thereafter paid no more attention to the masses than his predecessors had. His henchmen murdered anyone who spoke too openly against him, but at least this had the effect of terrorizing people into being peaceful. As a result, the haciendas became more productive and businesses were established. Belzú held office for eight years, a remarkably long time for Bolivia in the nineteenth century, and left the country hastily when he saw forces building up against him. The rapid succession of tyrants who followed in his wake could not entirely undo the benefits he had somewhat accidentally brought to Bolivia.

Bolivia's worst period came during the reign of terror under Mariano Melgarejo in the 1860s. Melgarejo believed force could gain him anything, and the three things he wanted were power, liquor, and women. He eliminated his enemies more regularly than Belzú had done, even killing them personally, yet he produced fear without bringing peace.

Trains were introduced into Bolivia early in the twentieth century. The locomotives, such as this one now displayed in Cochabamba, were usually small since they were brought to South America by ship and served on narrow-gauge lines

He was drunk much of the time, and his opponents kept hoping for a chance to kill him. On the international stage, he angered every country that bordered on his own and antagonized distant lands as well. One colorful tale reports he forced a British diplomat to ride out of La Paz naked on a burro. Where Bolivia didn't already have border disputes, he caused some, and in a senseless trade agreement with Brazil he as much as gave away about 50,000 square miles. He allowed Chileans to work the valuable nitrate deposits in the Atacama Desert belonging to Bolivia, paving the way for the loss of that entire region within a decade. Agustín Morales, who was anything but a great president, finally surprised Melgarejo with enough support to drive him from the country. While Melgarejo was living in exile, a relative of one of his lady friends caught up with him and shot him.

Conditions Improve

Before long Hilarión Daza gained control of the government. Though less vicious than either Belzú or Melgarejo, he ruled with cruelty and thoughtlessness. His period in office is of interest mainly because it saw the start of the "fertilizer war" that tore the Atacama Desert away from Bolivia and made the country a nation without a seacoast. After Daza met defeat in an early battle, Bolivia allowed Peru to do most of the fighting. Bolivian land and cities thereby escaped the period of occupation that Peru's had to suffer. In the treaty finally drawn up in 1904, Chile compensated for taking the desert region by agreeing to build a railway from Arica to La Paz over which Bolivia could freely ship her products to the coast. The line was finished in about eight years. Chile also paid Bolivia about $1,500,000 and made Arica a free port, doing away with the possibility of crippling trade duties. Bolivia feels less antagonism toward Chile than toward the United States in the matter of the mines and the seacoast lost. Like Peruvians, Bolivians think the States acted with greed when it supported Chile's claims. At the same time, Bolivia makes repeated demands today for a strip of land to give her a coast of her own. When Daza had to step down during the War of the Pacific, Bolivia's period of heartless, purposeless rule came to an end. Though leaders continued to come and disappear in brief,

A guard in his slightly frayed
uniform stands duty at the
Government Palace in La Paz,
which can be seen across the
plaza below. To the right, the
Cathedral has been witness to the
many revolts that have centered
around this square and the
Government Palace

incomplete terms of office, those that followed Daza usually had some concern for the nation's welfare.

As a result, after the "fertilizer war" Bolivia began to make slow progress. Life became relatively peaceful, though just before the end of the nineteenth century riots occurred over the location of the nation's capital. According to the constitution then in effect, Sucre was the legal seat of the government. But La Paz had outgrown Sucre and had also become the business center of the country. Many officials preferred to live in La Paz, which was replacing Sucre as the cultural heart of Bolivia and was more accessible to Peru. Finally, politicians decided the capital could exist in other centers besides Sucre and most government functions migrated to La Paz. On paper, Sucre remains the official capital, and the Supreme Court still has its headquarters there, but with its air and rail connections, La Paz today is the only city really prepared to act as the administrative heart of the nation.

The Twentieth Century

World War I brought Bolivia its first real chance for wide commercial development. Though she didn't declare war on Germany, her minerals served the Allies. After the war she continued to prosper until the worldwide depression caused her business partners to cut off orders for tin and other minerals. The country descended rapidly into a poverty-stricken condition once more. Bolivia's leaders hoped to improve the nation's commercial possibilities by opening an outlet to the Atlantic Ocean. (It was undoubtedly more than coincidence that she chose an area where prospectors hoped to discover oil.) For many years Bolivia had disputed with Paraguay over the territory at her southeastern corner, a region known as the Chaco, which included the navigable Paraguay River. Few Bolivians had moved into the area, while many Paraguayans had, but Bolivia decided old colonial boundaries entitled her to it. When Paraguay wouldn't withdraw, Bolivia sent armed forces into the region and at first they were victorious. International opinion also sided with Bolivia in the beginning. During the mid-1930s war over the area broke out anew, and this time the situation was reversed, both on the battlefield and in negotiations. Bolivia lost a large piece of territory.

Workers at the tin mine of Oruro, Bolivia. Tin continues to be a crucial source of income for the Bolivian economy, yet in the more primitive mines much work gets done by hand

Although she does have small ports on the Paraguay River, they are north of the easily navigated section and have proved of little value for commerce.

Throughout the nineteenth century and first third of the twentieth, political parties generally had little strength. Military rulers rather than parties carried power. In the 1940s, however, the *Movimiento Nacionalisto Revolucionario* (MNR) gathered a larger and larger following. While leaning toward the left, it also showed sympathies for groups of the far right, so much so that the Allies feared it might support Germany during World War II. Major Gualberto Villarroel, backed by the MNR, seized power during the war, but he allowed the tin barons to continue selling their mineral to the Allies. Nevertheless, he did attempt to reduce the power of the great tin-mine owning families—the Patiños, Aramayos, and Hochschilds. Under him the government also called for improved housing and working conditions for miners. It seems odd, since he appeared to be working for the people, that it was a mob uprising rather than a military one that removed him from office. The people shot him, then dragged him still alive into the square in front of the government buildings and hanged him. Some group stirred the mob to action, but no one has proven it was the Communists, as anti-Communists insist it was.

The Revolution That Mattered, Almost

The Nationalist Revolutionary Movement has been banned from time to time, but after each period of exile and underground existence, it has returned with new strength. In the election of 1951 Victor Paz Estenssoro ran as its presidential candidate, though he was in exile in Argentina. The MNR won, but a military junta quickly moved to take power and kept Paz Estenssoro from returning to La Paz. This brought on the one revolution in Bolivia, out of nearly two hundred uprisings, that meant more than just the exchange of one military leader for another. Students, laborers, and other people outside the army took part in this revolt, which made it possible for Paz Estenssoro to come home and fill the president's chair. Once in office, the new chief executive made changes that many officials ahead of him had promised or threatened to do. He nationalized the railroads and took over the tin mines. Although Bolivia had taken the local petroleum industry out of the hands of Standard Oil of New Jersey in 1937, that act had stemmed as much from anti-American feeling as anything else. The nationalization of the tin mines looked like an honest effort to help the country as a whole. Hacienda owners were forbidden to dispose of land and the Indians on it as though soil and people were one commodity. The government took idle acres from large haciendas for distribution among the landless, and some productive property as well. Paz Estenssoro permitted all men, regardless of whether or not they were literate and owned property, to vote. Women, too, received the right to use the ballot. The constitution still requires a man to be able to read and write and to own property to be able to vote, so at any time a president may go back to the old system.

How much did this revolution really do for the lower classes? The

Indians can now walk or sit in the main squares of any Bolivian city. Before 1952 they feared being shot if they did so. This seems to be a rather small advance considering Paz Estenssoro's feverish activity. But the tin mines had already produced their great yields, which probably explains why the tin barons, living comfortably in Europe and Chile, didn't put up more resistance. After World War II and the removal of the Japanese from southeast Asia, cheap tin from Indonesia caused a drop in price that practically slit Bolivia's throat economically. Laborers in the mines have received improved conditions at work and in housing, yet many of them appear to live much as they did before. They have taken less interest in expressing their wishes at the polls than had been hoped for, in part from ignorance, in part because Bolivian elections have long had a reputation for being dishonest, and in part because revolutions take the place of elections as often as not.

If the Indians were not part of the land when it was sold they had no place to go. Moving to the cities brought them exposure to

The prevalence of slum areas is one problem the Bolivian government has not yet managed to overcome, although efforts to improve conditions are being made

Campesinos are often misfits in the completely different life of the city. Even to the Bolivian city-dweller, this Indian of Tarabuco is inscrutable

more prejudice than they ever met on the altiplano and few chances to find work. Where the Indians were provided with land for the first time, they had no past experience in running a farm sensibly and more often than not wasted the new opportunity with which they had been presented. They have a reputation for laziness and dishonesty. When one becomes his own master, his laziness hurts himself, not an overseer or landlord, while stealing from oneself nets a man absolutely nothing. A great educational revolution is needed to prepare the Indians for the benefits from any type of change.

Little by little it grew obvious that the revolution had shortcomings. Some of the land made available to Indians lay in remote regions to which they had no desire to move. Haciendas broken up into hundred-acre farms produced less than they had when the land formed one large unit. Foreign technicians chased out of the mines and off the railroads had to be called back since Bolivia had few men capable of operating large industries. After the early changes, few more were instituted. Land distribution came to a halt, partly because the impoverished government wondered how it would ever make payment on the twenty-five-year bonds it gave in exchange for property, partly because of the unsatisfactory results where distribution had been carried out. Paz Estenssoro finally lost much of his popularity and gave up to a military junta in 1964, during his second term in office. The MNR, having once gained strength from the far right and the far left, now needed to reorganize and seek uniformity if it was to grow strong again.

Barrientos Takes Charge

Replacing Paz Estenssoro was René Barrientos Ortuño, a mestizo who spoke Quechua as well as Spanish and English. Once part of the MNR, he later seemed to be separated from parties and leaned toward the left. As a country, Bolivia faces farther left than most South American nations yet resists pressures from Russia and Cuba. This became especially obvious in 1967. A band of Communist guerrillas started stirring up trouble in the jungle south of Sucre early in the year. Perhaps there were fifty in the group, but Barrientos, seeking United States aid to finance resistance to them, made it sound as if they were swarming over half the country. As weeks of "hide-and-seek" maneuvers went on, Barrientos grew worried. But his concern was as much for himself as for the country. The failure of his troops to rid the jungle of the guerrillas gave his enemies a picture of weakness that he could not afford. After all, he was in control of the government on the strength of his military forces, and if they turned out to be ineffective against half a hundred guerrillas how could they possibly hold off an attempt to unseat him? To complicate the situation, the United States agreed to provide financial assistance only if Barrientos reduced waste spending. It may sound funny to an outsider that one of the poorest governments in the world has needless expenses, but this has always been one of the factors helping to keep the Bolivian treasury empty.

In April Barrientos got a break. His troops captured Jules Régis Debray, a wealthy Frenchman serving with the Communist guerrillas, and the president regained some of the prestige he had lost. Even so, police officers, businessmen, and the general public continued to fear an uprising of the Indians, which was what the guerrillas sought. It never came. Large numbers of the Indians, it appeared, wanted handouts. They weren't especially interested in struggling for advancement or change. When unrest did occur in the mines, Barrientos sent some of his soldiers into the state-owned mines in June to prevent serious incidents. They still occupied some of the mines in 1968, and union leaders complained they were there to prevent union elections and to frighten the workers into submissiveness. As 1967 wore on and many of the guerrillas continued to elude the government troops, Barrientos lost popularity once more. Word leaked out from Debray's jail that he was being confined under extremely uncomfortable conditions—in an "icy" cell—and that he had been brutally beaten. Barrientos needed a new victory of some sort, and it came in October.

Ernesto "Che" Guevara

The leader of the guerrillas, Ernesto "Che" Guevara, had been a close associate of Cuba's Fidel Castro and wanted to overthrow non-communist dictators in South American countries. Because Bolivia had such a huge group of impoverished masses, it seemed like a logical place to begin, but it turned out that the middle class rather than the lower classes leaned far left, and Guevara distrusted the middle class which didn't really want radical change. In October Barrientos' troops captured Guevara. Many reports have been issued on what happened next, but without doubt the guerrilla leader was shot within twenty-four hours. Bolivian officials at first tried to say he was shot during capture but newspapermen think he was taken without injury, questioned briefly, and then shot—possibly machine-gunned. He was probably shot in a schoolhouse, which may have been torn down to remove any signs of what had happened. His captors either cremated him or buried him in an unmarked grave, or both. Many mysteries may always surround his last day alive and his death, but his capture did much to restore Barrientos to favor in Bolivia.

In 1968 the last five survivors of Guevara's band turned up in Chile and surrendered. This made Bolivia and various other countries, particularly nearby Peru, fear that Chile might become a base for such guerrillas. Since Bolivia broke off diplomatic relations with Chile in

In La Paz, students marched with adults to protest the visit of five Russian parliamentarians to Bolivia

1962 because Chile would not give back part of the Atacama Desert, there is poor communication between the two countries. Instead of waiting to see if Bolivia would demand the return of the guerrillas, Chile ordered them out of the country. Before leaving Chile, the five admitted their mission had failed. Supposedly they went to Cuba, from where they could start over again once they were rested. Since the disbanding of Guevara's guerrillas, Communist terrorists in the nation have shifted their activities from rural areas to the cities. Instead of trying to rouse the Indians to revolt, they have endeavored to sabotage industries, shoot policemen, and frighten members of the upper classes.

As Bolivia Stands Today

Clearly Barrientos felt more secure with Guevara dead. When leaders of nearly all American nations had met in Uruguay in April, 1967, he didn't go. He gave as his excuse the fact that Bolivia's demands against

Chile for a strip of land to the Pacific had not been put on the program for discussion. But he may also have feared his government would be toppled while he was out of the country. When he refused to go, he didn't know Debray would be captured at about that time. But in July, 1968, he dared travel, making a "friendly" trip to the United States to pay a "social" call on President Lyndon B. Johnson in Texas. Texas was not new to him. He had received Air Force training there and was probably one of Bolivia's best pilots.

Barrientos preferred the cockpit of a plane to his desk at the presidential palace. His exploits in the air were legendary. In 1961, to disprove reports that three Bolivian paratroopers died because their chutes failed to open, he went to the airport, chose a parachute at random, and made a successful jump. Always traveling by air if possible he made frequent trips to rural areas. "I have the idea that every citizen must be a participant in building his country," he said. "In order to be a participant, he must know what the problems are and how they can be solved. In order to know, he must receive information and believe it. The destiny of telling the *campesinos* has fallen on me, a good friend of theirs."

In April, 1969, Barrientos arrived in the Andean village of Arque to dedicate a school named for John F. Kennedy. After the ceremony his helicopter took off from a basketball court, struck a power line, and crashed in flames killing a president who was revered by the *campesinos*. The greatest tribute to the stability of his government was the fact that the constitutional vice president, Luis Adolfo Siles-Salinas, assumed the presidency peacefully without interference from the military.

Bolivians are often resentful because their country today is but half the country it used to be. Every neighboring nation has taken land from Bolivia, until now it contains but 416,000 square miles—less than Alaska and about equal to Ontario in size. Once the third largest country in South America, today it is smaller than Peru (482,250 square miles), Colombia, Brazil, and Argentina. Many people in the lightly settled southern and eastern sections would like to secede and join Brazil or

Argentina, so Bolivia may have future problems about hanging onto land.

Outsiders seem to know less about Bolivia than about either Peru or Ecuador. So much has been said about the altitude that many people are afraid to visit the country. Reports have been exaggerated. A visitor should slow down, perhaps even rest, for an hour or two when he first arrives, but he does not have to take to bed for two days as "worriers" sometimes say. On the other hand, if he has breathing or heart trouble, he should be concerned about the altitude and consult his family doctor before going to the altiplano. It is not necessary to take thermal underwear to Bolivia. Days can be hot enough for only a sweater or jacket, and in resort areas such as Cochabamba shirt sleeves are sufficient when the sun shines, which it does much of the time. Ridges of high peaks hold back the clouds. From a plane you can look down and see masses of clouds lying along the mountains like a sea against a craggy coast. You feel you could walk out upon them as on a frozen lake covered with

The weather in Potosí was warm enough for jackets on this day. The laborer in the foreground wears a common type of suit, which resembles burlap, as he walks through one of the old thoroughfares of the city

Peace Corps volunteer Prudence Ingerman teaches arithmetic at a small school in La Paz, Bolivia

snow. But beyond the ridge not a cloud may be in sight. For a visit to Potosí, about two and a half miles high, warmer clothes are needed than if you plan to remain around La Paz, Sucre, Cochabamba, and Lake Titicaca.

Americans need not worry that people will run them off the streets shouting "Yankee, go home!" There is probably more anti-American feeling than in either Ecuador or Peru, but in those countries it is more out in the open. In Bolivia it remains under the surface. Bolivians don't want to run the risk of losing any advantages they may gain from seeming to be pro-American. Also, as long as power rests with a man like Barrientos who is to some extent pro-American, other officials and people will continue to hide their personal feelings to a degree. The fact that the Peace Corps remains in the country proves that Bolivians aren't likely to "bite" anybody. Peace Corps workers have not made as good an impression in Bolivia as in many other countries because they have a reputation for spending their time sight-seeing and because the real accomplishments they have made are minimized by leftists. It is difficult to judge the advances the Corps has truly made. Bolivia and Bolivians require a lot of study and "understanding." It makes one wonder if the United States or any other outsider has the patience to try to comprehend such a complicated nation.

Yesterday and Today in Ecuador

Antonio José de Sucre could have headed the first government in Ecuador after defeating Spanish forces in a battle about two miles above sea level on Mt. Pichincha. Instead, he continued to serve under Simón Bolívar in a drive to liberate all South America. Even had he stayed in Quito to govern, he would have been serving under Bolívar. The Venezuelan liberator had made plans to include Ecuador as part of Gran Colombia a year or more before the Quitu lands had been cleared of Spanish soldiers. The constitution Bolívar drew up for Colombia and Venezuela went into effect in Ecuador as soon as the country had been "freed." As Sucre carried Bolívar's fight for South American liberty into the highlands of Peru, Venezuelans, Colombians, and Englishmen from the liberating army remained in Ecuador to take control. The local Criollos must have felt little sense of liberation as they saw the government pass from one group of outsiders to another. For the Indians, any changes occurring were generally for the worse. Whereas officials from Spain had occasionally objected to harsh treatment of the native peoples, the new "conquerors" thought of them as animals. Landowners regularly mistreated the Indians as well as the thousands of Negro slaves who had been brought to the country to work in the tropical lowlands. Some Englishmen protested but soon met unpleasant deaths.

Among the outsiders who held power in Ecuador, the Venezuelan Juan José Flores enjoyed an especially strong position. After joining the armies of liberation while in his middle teens, he won Bolívar's

Following a tremendous earthquake in 1949, the Cathedral of Ambato, Ecuador, was restored with some modern and some old features

respect. As a result, he received command of the Gran Colombian forces in Ecuador a few years after Sucre drove the Spanish royalists from the area. Most of the men he trusted were from his own country or Europe. This kept him from winning popularity among the local people, and without Bolívar's backing he might never have risen to dictatorial heights. Ironically, he eventually broke with Bolívar to establish himself as master of Ecuador. It seems likely that he plotted the death of Sucre to be sure of controlling the country.

The Great Ones Fall

After leaving Bolivia, Sucre returned to Ecuador, where many Criollos remembered him as the hero of their struggle against Spain. He soon won further honors when he met an army led by Peru's president, José de La Mar, who had entered Ecuador to head off Bolívar's forces that were marching south to settle disturbances in Bolivia. Probably La Mar also hoped to make Guayaquil a part of Peru, since the city had often shown a desire to have closer ties with Lima than with Quito. By defeating the Peruvian invaders and helping to unify Ecuador, Sucre must have made Flores feel insecure. Nor was Flores pleased to have Sucre marry a girl of noble birth and settle in Quito to raise a family. Sucre, of all Bolívar's assistants, remained loyal to the great liberator. As long as Sucre stayed in Quito, Flores undoubtedly felt he should move cautiously in his plans to separate Ecuador from Gran Colombia.

Unrest came to Flores' assistance. Leaders in Venezuela and even in Colombia, right before Bolívar's eyes, drew away from the federation plan. Bolívar called on Sucre for aid once more, and the loyal general hurried to Bogotá, Gran Colombia's capital. There he presided over a congress that failed to produce harmony as Venezuela clearly indicated it wanted to go its own way. Bolívar, though Venezuelan by birth, could no longer enter his own country for fear of imprisonment. As the Liberator's representative, Sucre went to Venezuela but again had no luck in winning officials to Bolívar's point of view. Discouraged to see his dream of a United States of South America falling apart, Bolívar gave up all official titles in April, 1830, and prepared to struggle with his health problems. Unfortunately, he had tuberculosis and would die shortly before the year's end. Even at that, he outlived Sucre by six months. After his fruitless mission to Venezuela, Sucre started home to his wife and newborn daughter in Quito. The trip by horseback required several weeks and took the young general through wild, thinly populated mountains and jungles. No one knows who waited along his route. In a forest of southern Colombia about 150 miles northeast of Quito his lifeless body was found in June.

A Ruthless Caudillo

Very possibly Juan Flores had secret information about Sucre's assassination, but if so he kept it to himself. With the thirty-five-year-old Sucre dead and the forty-seven-year-old Bolívar dying, Flores, at the age of thirty, could establish himself as dictator of Ecuador and separate that country from Gran Colombia. He even tried to take the southern section of Colombia with him, but a short war forced him to see he wasn't as strong as he had hoped. His move to annex part of Colombia had some logic; both sides of the border were occupied by a single tribe of Indians which has ever since been split by the artificial boundary line. But Flores had no concern for the Indians. His interest was in gaining land, and the local peoples served merely as a convenient excuse. When he felt Colombia's might, he agreed to a border settlement and gave the Indians no further thought. To satisfy his territorial ambitions, he later claimed the Galápagos Islands, where the huge turtles gave him no resistance.

An uneducated mestizo, Flores faced the prejudice of Quito's aristocratic families. He found little revenue in the national treasury with which to buy favors, but he knew how to make extravagant promises or savage threats to gain his ends with the upper class. The promises he often broke once they had served his purposes, but he could be counted on to keep his threats. Men who sided with him received generous rewards as long as they never crossed him. His heavy tax program benefited his relatives and friends rather than the nation. For several years his forces prevented uprisings that would have disturbed the country's economic life. As a result, haciendas were productive and trade increased. But more and more men began to question the value of expanding their business affairs when the additional profits mostly went into Flores' pockets. Particularly in Guayaquil, Ecuador's main outlet to the Pacific and therefore the heart of the country's international trade, wealthy merchants looked about for another leader. Vicente Rocafuerte caught their attention. A writer who fought for freedom of the press when he wasn't in one of Flores' prisons, he appeared to be a good choice to lead a battle for all the personal liberties that were being suppressed. Besides, his family and friends already had wealth, so there appeared to be no reason for him to drain his backers of their money.

Rocafuerte willingly accepted leadership of the Guayaquil liberals. In a clash with government troops he met defeat, but he apparently frightened Flores. The president sought him out and made him certain promises. Mainly, Flores agreed to alternate with him as president every four years. According to this plan, Rocafuerte became head of Ecuador's government in 1835, though Flores remained in charge of

Ships of all sizes and types can be seen on the Guayas River at Guayaquil, Ecuador, which still remains the country's commercial hub

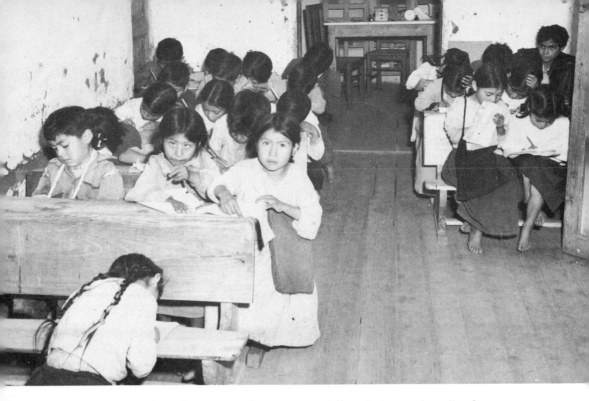

Primitive educational facilities stunt the progress of Ecuadorian society. In the village of Tambillo Viejo, children try to learn under crowded, poor conditions

the army and was a power behind the scenes. During his four-year term Rocafuerte brought about a few changes that improved conditions in the country. He had a new constitution written to replace a crude one drawn up by Flores, he used tax money for increasing educational facilities, he allowed political exiles to come home, and he lowered some taxes. As planned, he stepped aside in 1839 and Flores resumed control.

Briefly, it looked as if Flores had mellowed while watching the dignified Rocafuerte manage the government. Actually, Flores was just making sure he was firmly in power before imposing harsh rule on the land once more. He backed an uprising in southern Colombia, which cost Ecuador large sums of money and gained it nothing. To make up for the financial setback, he increased taxes. These made many people look forward to Rocafuerte's return to the presidency, but Flores ordered a new constitution thrown together that would let him continue as president for eight years. He offered Rocafuerte a handsome sum to "retire" from the country. Apparently Rocafuerte had lost his zeal for reform, for he accepted the settlement and moved to Paris. Flores probably did not realize how strong the Guayaquil liberals had grown. Showing that they could manage without Rocafuerte, they finally unseated Flores in 1845 and ordered him out of the country. Though it makes little sense, they agreed to pay him a pension while he lived in exile. Since he desired riches above all else, they probably hoped he would stay away if he had a steady income.

From Civil War to Civil War

For all his cruelty and stupidity, Flores had given Ecuador peace of a sort. For fifteen years after he left, the country existed in a state of civil war. Individuals and juntas appeared and fell so rapidly that each one averaged only a little more than a year in office. Both Colombia and Peru took advantage of the situation to try to capture bits of Ecuadorian territory, and some priests devoted more time to increasing the power and holdings of the Church than to conducting religious services. The liberals wanted the Church stripped of all power and fought to force it out of the government and to take over its lands. Only the Indians went on much as before, with little to lose and few hopes of gain. One leader did free the Negro slaves, which helped those people only slightly as long as the country remained in a state of upheaval. The Negroes who couldn't remain where they were usually joined an army for lack of anything else to do. As soldiers they received abusive treatment from their commanders and comrades and "got even" by mistreating civilians and enemies.

Finally, Ecuador seemed to be merely a group of armed city-states. Guillermo Franco saw more advantages to having his city, Guayaquil, be part of Peru than be part of such a divided Ecuador and agreed to a treaty to put much of southern Ecuador into Peruvian hands. Fright-

The Church has lost many of its holdings, but it is still ever-present in Ecuador. Here the attractive old San Francisco Church stands its ground among the modern buildings of Guayaquil

ened by this bold act, other cities forgot their differences and joined forces behind Gabriel García Moreno to block Franco's move. As García took control in Quito in 1860, he had a strong backer. His father-in-law, Juan José Flores, had returned from exile to help García gain the presidency. As it turned out, the son-in-law did not want advice from the former dictator. García could be quite ruthless, though no one was more sincerely religious than he. When Flores tried to become too powerful, García exiled him, and he soon died on a ship off the coast of Ecuador. Though a tyrant, García thought of his country whereas his father-in-law had thought mainly of himself. The younger man fostered education, stabilized the government and the national economy, improved transportation facilities, and allowed the Church to gain more power than the liberals had taken away from it. After his term of office ended, he managed two puppet regimes and regained control when the second puppet tried to shake loose from his grip. In 1875, just after he won an election for a new six-year term, his liberal enemies caught up with him and hacked him to death with a machete.

Once again Ecuador floundered through a period of civil war. García had given the conservatives such power that it took two decades for the liberals to become truly strong once more. During those twenty years they constantly stirred up trouble and toppled one government after

As part of Ecuador's educational planning program, an ultra-modern University City is intended to bring all departments of Central University together in Quito. Much of the construction is financed by outside sources, such as universities in the United States

another. The rulers who came and went averaged about three years apiece in office and had little chance to do anything for the nation. Much of the unrest originated in the southwestern corner of the country. Just as Arequipa became Peru's center of rebellion, Guayaquil proved to be fertile soil for discord in Ecuador. With promises of honest elections and stable government, the liberals gradually undermined the conservatives, most of whom lacked García's strict honesty and highly moral behavior. Besides, two decades gave the people time to get over the terrible fear they had felt for García and the Church during his fifteen years of government control. They wanted a change and believed Guayaquil's Flavio Eloy Alfaro would give it to them.

Liberal Rule

Alfaro's main contribution to the country was peace. He maintained it with brutality and dishonesty, but he maintained it. During each of his two terms, Alfaro had a new constitution written for the country, but no one in Ecuador was surprised at this. Rewriting the constitution had been a favorite "game" of presidents since the beginning of the republic. Even in the 1960s, after more than a dozen different constitutions, no one felt sure the "game" had ended.

During his first term in office Alfaro called for lessening the power of the Church. He snatched public education out of the hands of priests and nuns and confiscated Church lands. Alfaro's actions created an "education gap" that could not be closed for several years, for Ecuador, like all Latin American countries, needed more educational facilities and teachers, not less. The people who benefited during his reign were businessmen and holders (other than the Church) of large estates. Because he crushed revolts before they disrupted the country, trade could be carried on with some degree of security. New roads and railroads allowed manufacturers and farmers to ship products more easily than had been possible before. Haciendas produced fairly steadily, since they escaped serving as battlefields; however, many of the landlords preferred to live outside the country while the untrustworthy Alfaro held the presidency, leaving overseers to look after their interests.

At the end of his first six-year term, Alfaro arranged for Leónidas

113

Plaza Gutiérrez to take control. Plaza Gutiérrez proved to be more than a puppet. Though he continued Alfaro's road- and railroad-building programs, he also built schools and in other ways aided education. However, he did not put public education back in the hands of religious orders, for he was as anticlerical as most other Ecuadorian liberals of his day. Telephone and telegraph services grew during the years Plaza Gutiérrez held office. He, too, kept the country peaceful. Toward the end of his six-year period in office he showed an inclination to hang onto the presidency, creating a rift between himself and Alfaro. Apparently Plaza Gutiérrez decided against risking open conflict, for he stepped down and Alfaro once more filled the presidential chair.

Alfaro's program was much as before, with a highlight of his second term being completion of a badly needed rail line between Quito and Guayaquil. He did more for education than previously. While he was in office the second time, the world market for cacao, used in making chocolate, expanded. As a cacao producer, Ecuador profited, and delighted hacienda owners gave Alfaro much of the credit. Actually, the main thing he did, as before, was to keep the peace, which allowed agriculture and business to flourish. As his six-year term ran out, he proved even less willing than Plaza Gutiérrez had been to give up the presidency. Open conflict could no longer be avoided, and in the revolt that followed, Plaza Gutiérrez came out victorious and threw Alfaro into prison. A mob later broke into the penitentiary—perhaps the guards had instructions to let it happen—and hacked Alfaro to death before setting his body afire. Plaza Gutiérrez completed a four-year term (as called for by the new constitution) and passed the presidency on to another liberal.

Plaza Gutiérrez was the greater of the two and probably did more for Ecuador, yet Eloy Alfaro is the man recalled today as an outstanding hero. His flamboyant, danger-filled career appeals to Latin Americans.

Declining Fortunes

If cacao had remained profitable, liberal presidents might have followed one another in reasonably peaceful succession. Unfortunately, a fungas disease known as witches'-broom attacked the cacao trees. Planta-

Ecuadorian industry develops slowly, but the jungles of the country provide plenty of wood for lumbering. Along the Guayas River, the logs are floated to Guayaquil in huge rafts

tion laborers and overseers either paid little attention as brushy growths developed on the trees or else waited for instructions from landlords who were living abroad, especially in Europe. When buyers started rejecting Ecuadorian cacao, people realized something should be done, but by then the disease had spread throughout much of the country. Just as Alfaro had received credit for the cacao prosperity that he didn't really create, presidents during the cacao collapse of the 1920s took the blame for the new change in fortunes. Revolts and threats of revolts became more numerous. When the world depression of the 1930s struck, upsets became so commonplace that more than a dozen presidents served during a period of ten years. At the same time, Ecuador became a gathering place for pro-Nazi Germans, who stirred up hatred against France, Great Britain, and especially, the United States.

A Police State

Ecuador might have suffered during World War II instead of profiting like her neighbors had not Carlos Alberto Arroyo del Río come to power in 1940. He established a police system that was really a type of Gestapo—the Nazi secret police of Germany who guarded against anti-government activities. At the same time, to show he was not pro-

German, he took the local airline out of the hands of German officers and pilots and turned it over to an American company. After the United States entered World War II, Arroyo severed diplomatic relations with Germany, Italy, and Japan and allowed Americans to use the Galápagos Islands for sea and air bases. By being friendly with the Allies, Ecuador's president made it possible for his country to sell them lightweight balsa for use in planes and cinchona bark for use in anti-malarial drugs, such as quinine. At the same time, American technicians gave a hand in fighting the witches'-broom disease so the cacao industry made something of a comeback.

It soon became obvious to Ecuadorians that Arroyo was catering to American interests in hopes they would support him in office, which they did. This added to the anti-American feeling that the pro-Nazi Germans in the country had already stimulated. To make matters considerably worse, Peru chose this time to invade a large area of southern Ecuador over which there had long been a dispute about ownership. Though his police force was strong, Arroyo had it scattered throughout the cities and dared not call it together to serve as an army. His fighting forces were weak, and they fell back before the Peruvian troops. When a conference of ministers from North and South American countries met in Brazil in 1942, it recognized Peru's ownership of the disputed land, which naturally infuriated Ecuadorians. They claimed the United States had dominated the meeting and was therefore to blame, so anti-American feeling increased. If a mistake was made, which seems possible, Brazil and Colombia were as much at fault as anybody. Colombians and Brazilians had snatched generous chunks of land away from Ecuador early in the twentieth century. To keep that issue from being brought up, they inclined toward Peru's claims rather than to Ecuador's. All this land grabbing left Ecuador with about 100,000 square miles—roughly the size of Wyoming—and made it one of the smallest countries of South America.

Despite loss of favor, Arroyo held on. He probably would have completed his four-year term if he had been willing to permit honest elections as he promised. Instead, he maneuvered to place a puppet in the presidency when his term neared its end. In a well-planned massacre, military rebels killed hundreds of his policemen, leaving him with little backing. José María Velasco Ibarra, who had held office for a year in the 1930s, came home from exile to try his luck at governing once more. He claimed to be a leftist but soon angered other leftists and found himself relying on the conservative politicians for his strength. Whatever he was or pretended to be, he brought thirty years of liberal rule to an end. The Indians listened to his grand promises and hoped for a little improvement. They had failed to gain much under the liberals, who claimed to be protecting them by saving them from domination by the Church and from alcoholism.

From Velasco to Velasco

Velasco seemed to rule by confusing the opposition. At one moment he appeared to have Nazi inclinations, at another to be Communistic; he borrowed liberal tactics where they served him and used the conservatives when necessary. He called for a constitution that everyone knew would prove unworkable, and when it was written, tried to get out of signing it. Handing out tributes to anyone who flattered him, he caused men under him to distrust one another while they scrambled for his favors. He reportedly would tell one official to do a certain thing and another official to do exactly the opposite, with the result that nothing got done. At first men thought this was due to muddled thinking. In time some began to wonder if it wasn't a well thought out ruse. He could make lavish promises to the masses and then blame his subordinates when the promises weren't carried out. No one could deny he made a colorful president. His fiery speeches made all other candidates and officials sound like weaklings. The people loved him as a result. "Give me a balcony," a newspaperman quoted him, "and I could be elected president anywhere." But the military thought less highly of his shenanigans. Three years after he took office in 1944, army officers kicked him out.

In less than twelve months he was followed by three more presidents, but then a most unusual man—a man who really tried to keep his political promises—stepped into the presidency. This was Galo Plaza Lasso, a son of Leónidas Plaza Gutiérrez. Of course, it takes more than

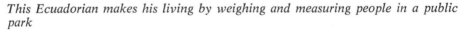
This Ecuadorian makes his living by weighing and measuring people in a public park

one man to keep political promises, and much of what Plaza tried to do was wasted effort. Officials disregarded his requests, or the congress failed to support his measures, or there was no money in the treasury with which to make his improvements. Besides, he spent more time finding out what was holding Ecuador back than in pushing it forward. He called in specialists and technicians, especially from the United States, and asked them to study everything from government expenditures to agricultural practices as a step toward replacing inefficient activities with practical ones. Reams of reports stacked up in his office and on the desks of cabinet ministers. The next president and his assistants found them there, gathering dust. However, the country knew four years of peace, during which the banana industry developed rapidly. When his term neared its end, he left it to the people to choose his successor instead of trying to force his candidate on them. And the people's choice was once more Velasco Ibarra.

Though unpopular with the military, the Church and the rest of the aristocracy—it is said, "Nobody likes Velasco but the people"—he managed to last his four years. Rather than take a chance on having an "accident," he left the country as soon as his term was over, but returned after another four years and won election for the fourth time. Army officers unseated him a year later, and this time he had to wait nearly eight years before the 1968 election placed him in power once more. He ran for the presidency from outside the country about as often as from within, but the people did not forget him between elections. While in exile, he taught law at various universities—now in Chile, again in Argentina—and was eagerly sought as a colorful speaker. When in Ecuador, he did no more for the poor than other rich leaders had done. But his background was middle class rather than aristocratic, and the masses were impressed by this. Also, as one Ecuadorian told a reporter, " . . . it really doesn't matter who the president is. But . . . Velasco makes the people up there [in the government] uncomfortable. So they [the masses] vote for him. It is the only way they have to protest."

A Glance at Ecuadorian Politics

Much of what any president does in office has political overtones. Each man seems more concerned with staying in power or returning to power later than in making notable changes. When Otto Arosemena Gómez demanded that the United States recall Ambassador Wymberley deR. Coerr in October, 1967, he gave the reason that Coerr had shown disrespect for local authority. Actually, Coerr was standing up for the Alliance for Progress, which Arosemena had been attacking. Arosemena was crying for more United States aid for Latin American countries, especially for Ecuador. If he got more aid, he might stand a good chance of picking the next president of his country. Instead, Coerr reported on the way Ecuador wasted aid money and did almost nothing to help itself. This hurt Arosemena's prospects, so he got Coerr recalled though he didn't break diplomatic relations with the States. Coerr's removal did not help Arosemena's prospects, as it turned out. This is just one example of the political maneuvering that goes on while millions of people fare no better than they did before.

Elections in Ecuador are usually accompanied by some disorders if not outright violence. For instance, during the 1968 election, students held demonstrations in the main public park of Guayaquil on election night. They heckled the police who had closed off an adjoining block where one of the political candidates was staying. Finally the officers chased the youths away with a mild tear gas. Crowds of students and curious onlookers fled, sneezing, blowing their noses, and wiping their eyes, but before long they returned. After being chased by the police a few times, the students decided they had made enough of a disturbance and disbanded. (An hour later, amorous couples, some of the students among them, occupied the benches in the area earlier cleared by the police.) Had really important issues been at stake, there might have been open clashes, with bashed heads and many arrests. All the police wore riot helmets and were otherwise prepared for serious trouble.

One of the issues to contend with in Ecuador is poverty. Here a single faucet provides water for dozens of families in a slum section of Guayaquil, which is estimated to be more than sixty per cent slums

120

*In contrast to the slums, one notes the luxury hotel of Ecuador—the Quito—
one of the most attractive hotels of all South America*

An outsider cannot help but wonder if many of the people who vote
in Latin American elections understand what an election is all about.
In 1967 in the town of Picoaza, Ecuador, a rather strange thing happened during a mayoralty election. A company that produces a foot
powder called Pulvapies decided to cash in on interest in the election
by using the slogan "Vote for any candidate, but if you want well-being
and hygiene, vote for Pulvapies." The night before the election, the
company handed out advertising leaflets that resembled official ballots.
These said, "For Mayor: Honorable Pulvapies." So many people de-
posited these leaflets in the ballot boxes the next day that the foot
powder won the election. If it had happened as a joke, it would be
rather funny; but reports say that a great many people didn't understand why the election had to be held again, and that makes it somewhat tragic.

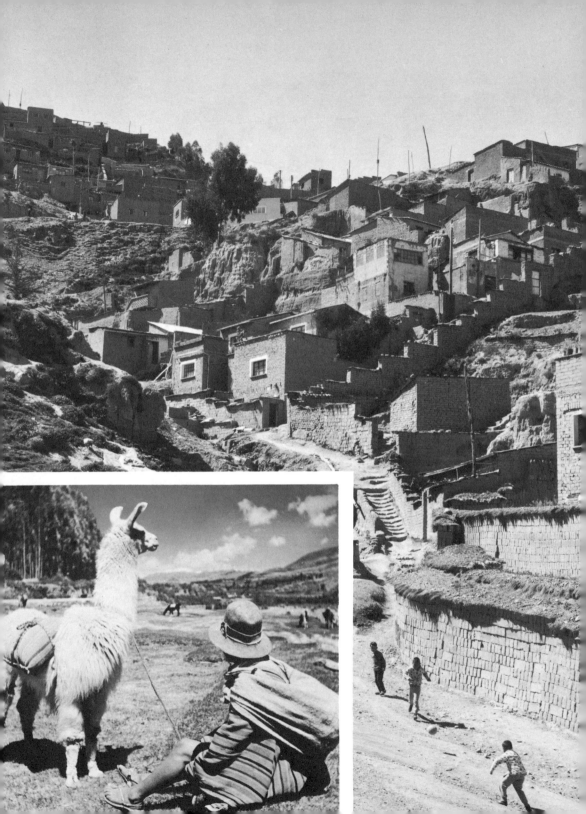

On the Campo, In the City

On the altiplano and in valleys far from cities like Lima, La Paz, and Quito, thousands of Indians follow a life similar to that of the days when the Pizarros arrived in Peru. Women make bread from coarse wheat or corn flour, or a combination of the two; grow potatoes, beans, squash, and avocados; and tend flocks of goats or sheep. Men help with the heaviest farm work and assist in planting, cultivating, and harvesting when these amount to more than the women can handle. On market days a man carries produce for sale to the nearest village, managing a load so heavy he may be unable to lift it off the ground without help. His wife stands behind the load as he sits, squats, or kneels with his back against it. She hands him ropes or strips torn from an old blanket and helps him to adjust them around the bundle of produce and his chest. When he leans forward to rise, she grabs the bundle and lifts, making it possible for him to get to his feet with the load balanced on his back. If he stands too straight, the weight may pull him over backward, while if he leans too far forward, it could topple him nose-first into the dirt. But once he has it properly balanced, he can carry it for miles without help.

The farther out on the *campo*—the open country—they live, the earlier families start for the market place. As they trudge toward the village, which may be a few to a dozen miles away, they meet other Indian families along the dusty trails their bare feet have worn across the fields and pastures. As often as not, an entire family goes to the village on market day. Older girls and boys may help carry loads,

An Andean farm lad experiences a different life from his counterparts in the city, who play soccer on a steep hillside of La Paz

123

though they don't weigh themselves down the way grown men do. Each family usually goes single file, with the man of the household leading the group. Older girls take much of the responsibility in keeping track of the younger children during the long hike. But the mother is not idle. She often has a baby tied in a blanket riding on her back, while her hands keep busy spinning a mass of wool she carries. She maintains a smooth gait and jostles her baby only a little. If he starts to fret, she shrugs and twitches her shoulders to joggle and rock him from side to to side. The head of a very small baby bounces back and forth as though he had no bones in his neck. If he continues to cry, the mother feeds him.

The Women

Mothers carry babies until they reach the age of three or so, because very small children would be unable to keep up with the family. With long distances to cover, no one has the time or patience to wait on a dawdling two-year-old. Of course, the arrival of a new baby forces an older one to start walking, or else the older one rides on the back of a teen-age sister. Girls, considered comparatively worthless alongside boys, are made to walk at an earlier age than boys. Yet, more often than not, girls and women keep Indian families alive and functioning. Women do more than half the work, including some of the heavy labor as well as cooking, herding, spinning, and weaving. The men usually put forth their greatest effort when they hire out to work rather than when they work for themselves. If trouble crops up, the men often disappear and get drunk, leaving the women to face whatever problem has arisen.

Indian women throughout the central Andes countries wear colorful clothes. The blanket in which a baby rides is almost always striped, while a blanket that a woman wears to keep herself warm is more likely to be of a solid color. In addition to blankets, women wear shawls and blouses, petticoats and brightly colored skirts. On an ordinary day a woman will have on two or three skirts over two or more petticoats. She may wear up to thirty skirts at once in addition to a few petticoats on a feast or other special day. Sometimes she will be

Women of the Peruvian altiplano

unable to walk without assistance when she gets into all her clothes, but few of the Indian women can afford to own more than half a dozen skirts. After sunset and during the cooler season, several layers of clothing help keep a person warm. But a woman may also wear all she has to make sure they won't be stolen while she's away from home. Most Indian women on the altiplano wear hats, ranging from derbies to stovepipes. The women of Peru and Ecuador appear to prefer small, round-topped hats, while Indians of Bolivia like tall ones. Observers who have studied Indian dress closely say they can tell where a woman is from by the type of hat she wears. For instance, Indian women around Cochabamba, Bolivia, appear mostly in wide-brimmed, high-topped straw hats painted white. Sometimes these are fancily decorated

125

In their high white hats, Bolivian women sell grains at the market in Santa Cruz

with a thin strip of black ribbon. When freshly painted, they gleam in the sunlight almost like enamel, but after many months of wear or a few rainfalls, unless they are painted anew, they clearly show that they are made of closely woven brown straw.

The Men

The Indian man dresses somewhat like a businessman, wearing trousers and a shirt, with a jacket added when he wants more warmth or to look dressed up. He may cover his shoulders with a blanket on cold or rainy days and often wears a hat. Certain regions and certain groups have distinctive dress, of course. Indian laborers in southern Bolivia can be seen in suits that appear to be made of burlap. The jackets of these are short and close-fitting, while the pants legs end anywhere between the knee and the ankle. The older Yagua Indians along the Amazon River stick to clothing made of grass hanging from cords passed around the body. Yagua witch doctors wear face and body makeup. They break open the pods of achiote plants and crush the seeds inside to make a red paste with which to streak their skin. The male Colorado Indians of Ecuador also use this paste, matting their hair with it until they appear to have red bowls upside down on their heads. These men wear skirts of striped cloth as they tend their banana, cacao, pepper, and cassava crops. They occasionally hunt monkeys for food but more often eat pigs and chickens raised on their farms.

The Children

While older Indians stick to traditional dress, their children are breaking away from it. On the altiplano the poorest older woman tries to have one clean, colorful, well-kept blanket to wear on special occasions. Her teen-age daughter or granddaughter may refuse to wear a blanket at any time. Although the girls are generally keeping the full, flaring skirts, they are substituting sweaters and jackets for blankets and shawls. They no longer go barefooted and may even clothe their legs in loosely woven or patterned stockings. Instead of wearing derby or stovepipe hats, they go with their jet-black, glossy hair uncovered.

Farm youths wear a burlaplike suit to work in the fields. The boy on the left also wears a knitted cap, a lluchu, which is very popular in this area

A Quechua Indian child of Peru keeps warm in a poncho and a chullo *(cap), the colorful handiwork of his people*

Some young women no longer settle for trailing behind their men but walk abreast of them, and those especially influenced by city ways will even be seen walking hand in hand with their boy friends. Among the jungle peoples, who see less of outside styles, the younger generations are also giving up the old ways. Young men of the Yaguas often dress in slacks and sport shirts instead of grass skirts, and even small boys may prefer cotton shorts to going naked.

Otavalo Indians

For the most part, the poor Indians accept modern ways more slowly than those who manage to save a little money. As in other societies, the Indians have their poor, their middle class, and their upper classes. But with few exceptions, a well-to-do Indian is poorer than a lower-middle-class white man. Notable exceptions are found among the Otavalo Indians of Ecuador. These Indians have refused to intermarry with whites or other peoples and are often considered to be among the most handsome natives of the central Andes. They also enjoy a reputation for being the cleanest. Every morning about five o'clock they go to the nearest lake or stream to bathe before dressing in their distinctive white loose-fitting clothes. The men wear their hair neatly braided down their backs. Working industriously, these Indians produce beautiful ponchos, scarves, and, in the region of Cuenca, Panama hats. Most Otavalos look well fed. Instead of spending more than they can afford on liquor, they eat sensibly. They even manage to save some of their earnings, which places them among the upper classes of Indian societies.

Because city dwellers and tourists are the best customers for their woven goods, the Otavalo Indians stay in close contact with white people. But they do not lug their produce to a market and sit for hours with dozens or hundreds of other people offering the same items. They stay on their feet, venturing up one street and down another in the better sections of town to seek out possible buyers. A woman who might never get to a market may be glad of the chance to purchase a scarf from a man passing her front gate.

Otavalo Indian women weave the famous "Panama" straw hats

Woven mats for sale at a market in Riobamba, Ecuador. Some will be used as rugs on dirt floors, but others will be the only beds in the huts of the very poor. Below, sandals produced from old tires are among the wares of a Bolivian Indian market

At the Market

Other Indians behave quite differently. Especially on the altiplano, they go to market areas and crowd together, squatting on street curbs or the ground, while waiting for customers. In almost every market similar goods are sold together. All the people with pottery will occupy one block or corner, those with garden vegetables will be together in another location, and women with clothing to sell will be bunched in a third place. A particularly industrious woman calls her wares occasionally, but most sit silently making no apparent effort to conclude a sale. A few bring enough wool to be able to spin while they wait, and ambitious ones may knit sweaters as the hours pass. If a store sells the sweaters she knits or provides her with the wool, most of the money goes to the store. If she uses her own wool and sells the garment herself, she usually asks about six dollars and feels she has made a fair profit.

Being tired after their long walks from their farms, some women doze. Chatting helps pass the time at the markets, and Indian women enjoy gossip. The Aymaras, more than others, delight in jokes and playful scuffling. They give one another silly names which, though insulting, are usually funny enough to prevent hard feelings. If a man's feet fly out from under him because he steps in some animal droppings, he is more likely to be laughed at than helped to get up. If a boy looks fondly after a girl, he will surely be teased, while the girl can count on jokes at her expense if she gives him any encouragement. Away from the markets the Aymaras sing softly or hum, but they remain subdued, even appearing downcast, when white strangers are around. The casual observer shouldn't jump to the conclusion that they or any of the Indians are truly happy or contented. It is difficult to be really happy while they need food and an easier, more pleasant way of life. Much of the time they struggle too hard to be either cheerful or sad, and their faces often reflect nothing more than resignation. However, joking and scuffling, among women as well as men, breaks the monotony of their days.

While a mother sits at a market, her children may stray from sight. If she feels concern, she seldom shows it. Indian children become self-sufficient soon after they learn to walk, and most of them run about village and city streets with as much confidence as teen-agers. A child who stays away too long may be spanked by his father when he returns to the market, especially if he causes the family to get a late start back to the campo. Many parents, though, scold instead of using violence. This is a recent thing. Less than a quarter of a century ago Indian parents beat their children. If they lived on haciendas, adults frightened youngsters by saying the *patrón,* or owner of the land, would punish children who misbehaved. Some hacienda owners did whip or otherwise punish grown men and possibly youngsters. Both young people and their parents feared the *patrón.* With his gradual tempering or disappearance, especially since Bolivia's revolution of 1952, the *patrón* no longer serves as a threat to mischievous children. And many fathers, remembering how they hated severe punishments at the hands of the *patróns,* refrain from spanking their children.

Back to the Campo

Most markets begin to close down before evening. *Campesinos*—people from the campo—with long distances to go start home early. Particularly on the high altiplano, the air becomes chilly as the sun sets. Travelers from low regions may not suffer especially, as their blood has not adapted to the conditions of high places and it helps keep them warm. But Indians who have lived all their lives on the altiplano really feel the cold. That is why a woman can wear many clothes all day long. In order to get home while the sun still provides some warmth, Indians put up their unsold goods and set off across the campo. To help them feel warm, they probably chew coca leaves and lime. Coca has been called the "central heating of the altiplano," but the lime is necessary to bring out the full narcotic effect of the leaves. The drug stirs the circulation and makes the chewer feel warm. It also kills pain, making him oblivious to aching muscles or the sensation of hunger. Miners, instead of having a break for tea in the afternoon, have a coca break. The leaves can be bought openly at certain markets, frequently those where smuggled goods are also freely displayed. In time the narcotic affects the brain, after which a person can carry on little if any

132

productive work. He goes about as though in a stupor, eyes half closed, unable to concentrate on any purpose in life.

Up Goes a House

In addition to producing much of his own food and clothing, the Indian builds his own house. The jungle dweller uses poles, leaves, and grass to make a simple hut. On the altiplano and the coastal desert, Indians use sun-dried mud and adobe for building materials. Because adobe comes from a clayey earth, it holds up better during a rain than ordinary mud, but where these materials are used, rainfall generally is scant. Few people build a house entirely by themselves. Relatives, friends, and neighbors help out, forming a *minga,* which is similar to an old-fashioned American barn-raising work party. On the altiplano when a *campesino* builds a new house, he buys four llama embryos, which are sold at certain shops or markets, and buries one in a hole under each corner of the building. Then the members of the *minga* drink liquors that come in five to seven different colors. The Indians claim that if you drink them in the proper sequence (which is why it is necessary for them to have separate colors), you don't get drunk. But if you mix the order, you'll end up falling on your face. Once the drink-

High on a mountainside in La Paz, capital of Bolivia, a man digs up his backyard to make adobe bricks, the common building material of the altiplano

133

In his backyard in the village of Tiahuanaco, Bolivia, a man grows grass for thatched roofs and also digs up part of the land to make adobe bricks

ing ceremony has been performed, a band plays, the womenfolk start roasting a whole pig and fixing other delicious foods, and the men of the *minga* stack up adobe tiles to form the walls. When the time comes to put on the roof, the family buys baskets of flowers to hang from the eaves and from other parts of the roof as it goes up.

All during the building process much feasting and drinking goes on, and the band may come to play several times. Some families spend so much on the celebration, the embryonic llamas, and the baskets of flowers that they run out of money and are unable to complete the house. It may stand partially built for months until they save enough money to finish paying for materials needed. In the meantime they live elsewhere, probably with close relatives. Unless people use thatch, a roof is the most expensive part of a house. If a man owns the land on which he builds, he can make his own adobe tiles by digging up part of his lot. Even adobe bought from friends or relatives does not break a man. But a tile or metal roof must be purchased from a dealer and proves expensive for an Indian family of small means. A door, doorframe, and windowframes would also be costly, since the altiplano lacks trees, and wood must be shipped in. Frequently the door is simply an opening over which a blanket hangs, and windows, if included at all, are the same. Before he worries about dressing up his house with non-essentials like windows or wooden doors, a *campesino* spends his spare cash for three necessities. He buys a transistor radio (lacking electricity, he can use no other kind), a bicycle, and a sewing machine.

Most houses are one story high. Under the influence of missionaries, some Indians in the past built two-story homes, but these made little sense on the campo where there is plenty of space for all rooms of a building to be on the ground level. Many Indians came to fear that the higher houses would be hit by lightning more easily than one-story buildings. People of the altiplano, even when they follow Christian beliefs, often cling to their old theory that the devil is up and God is down. They "know" this because lightning and storms come from above, while food grows up from the earth. When a house is hit by lightning, no one lives in it for over a year. The family plants a tree in front of it, and after a certain time has passed, children, who represent innocence, dance around the tree. After that, the family can move back in.

The Big Move

More and more Indian and mestizo families are moving to towns and cities. In Peru the people have been leaving the country since the early 1950s, but the migration to urban areas in Bolivia and Ecuador is much more recent. About two-thirds of Peru's people lived in rural areas in 1950, while in the late 1960s estimates reported that more than half of all Peruvians could be found in towns and cities. By contrast, about three-fourths of the people in Ecuador and Bolivia lived in the country in the early 1950s. A decade and a half later the population in rural areas had fallen to slightly less than two-thirds of each country's total. In all countries, but especially in Peru, farm machines have taken the place of laborers. Shunted off farms and haciendas, the displaced people seek their fortunes in the cities but without any preparation for a

Japanese immigrants arrive in Santa Cruz, Bolivia, to take part in a colonization project sponsored jointly by Japan and Bolivia. Aided by their own government, they will have little contact with the local population but will retain their distinctiveness as they cultivate land which has not been previously farmed

changed way of life. Lacking special skills and often without an education, the migrants settle for hard work at low pay. If they don't already know how, they quickly learn to beg and steal. This would be less necessary if people already in the settlements spent as much effort in helping the newcomers to adjust and find work as they spend in trying to protect property or bring culprits to justice.

The more a person shows his Indian heritage, the more likely he is to suffer. Although some estimates say Bolivia's population is two-thirds Indian, recent United Nations statistics put the figure at nearer 55 per cent. This gives the country the highest ratio of Indians to whites of any nation in South America. In Peru the Indian peoples make up 40 to 45 per cent of the total population, and in Ecuador estimates rank about 40 per cent of the people as Indians. Another 40 per cent of Ecuadorians are classed as mestizos, while about that same number of Peruvians and 30 per cent of Bolivians are of mixed Indian and white blood. In each country between 10 and 15 per cent of the people are white, and probably less than 5 per cent are Negroes and Asiatics. In spite of their overwhelming numbers, the Indians and mestizos face considerable prejudice. Some movie houses will not sell tickets to Indians, and there are hotels that never have rooms when these people come in. Mestizo women get positions as servants more easily than the Indians as a rule. Some mestizos consider themselves superior to Indians, as do some Negroes, and the Asiatics usually look down on Negroes, mestizos, and Indians. Even the Indians who have established themselves in the cities and have steady, though poor, incomes may avoid associating with the displaced persons just in from the campo. Yet on the streets, people mingle fairly freely, and prejudice is not usually obvious.

A street scene in Quito, Ecuador, where people wait to take advantage of a bargain sale

A Middle Class

The well-to-do people, who are almost all white, hide their prejudices better than those in the middle classes, probably because the wealthy are an old, established group with long experience in masking their thoughts. None of the three countries has a large middle class, but in each region one is growing slowly. Poor people who persevere until they get an education can work their way into the middle class through sticking to office jobs, opening small shops, or winning respect in industrial enterprises. But great numbers of the poor will not make an effort to get an education, will not stay with a job once they've found it, and will not be reliable enough to win anyone's respect. Most middle-class groups can be found in the capital cities, where government jobs are available, and in such industrial or commercial centers as Guayaquil, Arequipa, and Cochabamba. Bolivia has a new group developing along the Argentine border where oil has been discovered and is gradually being exploited. As soon as a family rises above the lower classes, it hires at least one servant.

Young People of the City

All young people have certain obligations in the family, even after servants take over much of the household work. Obedience to parents is one of the main features of good manners in the central Andes, and so, grumbling in protest, boys and girls usually do the chores required of them. Young people show respect for their parents by being on time for meals and other family gatherings and by going places with the adults. A few teen-age boys are beginning to show signs of rebellion. They feel too many social customs linger from Spanish times, and they envy the freedom of young people in nearby Chile. Some anger their parents by treating their homes like hotels, coming and going as they please with no consideration for family timetables. Yet no parent in the middle or upper classes would think of punishing a child. It has been said, and not entirely as a joke, that among upper-class families a man is more likely to strike his wife than his child.

Young men as well as girls live at home until they marry, and even then many couples live with one set of parents. The father who can afford it expects to look after the needs of all his children until they marry even though they may be grown and have jobs of their own. He buys their clothes, takes care of family laundry, supplies all food, and never expects either a son or daughter to help with household expenses unless misfortune forces him to it. A young man with a job provides his own money for such luxuries as movies, snacks, and soccer games but otherwise allows his father to worry about the family's financial needs. Once he marries, the young man takes on some of the financial responsibilities in the home where he lives and probably looks after all of them when he sets up his own household.

Between the ages of twelve and fifteen a boy must start proving he is a man. He begins to smoke, if he didn't start at a younger age, and to drink. An older boy or man, quite often his father, introduces him to women of the town and pays for his visits to them. At about the same time, he looks around for a girl from a respectable family to date. He

Promenading on Sunday after church remains popular along the major boulevard of La Paz. People fortunate enough to have cars drive round and round in order to be seen in them

generally meets several at family parties among the friends of his parents, and when he asks one for a date, he expects to go steady with her. She and her family supposedly think nothing of his other activities, for they are the traditional way of life, and he would be considered peculiar if he avoided them. Then *he* would be avoided. In Peru girls try to date boys older than themselves. Throughout the countries of the central Andes, a boy and girl go steady from the first date. No casual dating of one person and then another is permitted among respectable families. Until she is about sixteen, a girl receives fairly close supervision. She invites the boy to her home, promenades in a park with him and members of her family, or accompanies him to movies with groups of mutual friends. In spite of being with other people, young couples find plenty of opportunities for holding hands, kissing, and pretending to be seriously in love. If one tires of the other, he breaks off the romance and finds another steady friend. In fact, the next steady has probably already been located before the old one gets his freedom.

In Bolivia and to a lesser extent in Peru and Ecuador young men still serenade their girl friends. If a boy sings badly or cannot play the guitar, which is rare, he may hire musicians to play or sing at his girl friend's house. But the modern trend finds him standing under her window with his transistor radio turned up to full volume. A few boys and girls date but one person throughout their teens and marry that person. This happens particularly in rural areas, where young people marry at sixteen or seventeen, sometimes at fifteen or fourteen. Most city boys and girls change steady friends a few times before they finally settle down, between the ages of nineteen and twenty-five, to get married. Boys of good family are expected to finish a university course before they wed. Though the courtship may be long, the engagement will usually be short.

About the only things that keep young people from seeking romance are lack of money and a strong desire for an education. Even the girl must have money to be popular much of the time. Of course, she never helps out with expenses on a date, for going Dutch treat is practically unheard of. And a girl rarely puts an education ahead of her social life. Her father must have enough money to buy her clothes and cosmetics and to allow her to give parties in the home. There are few dances, plays, and the like to which young people can go in Bolivia, Ecuador, and Peru, so much of the social life takes place in the family circle. Every girl expects to be able to entertain groups of her girl friends as well as groups of couples. Parties for just boys, however, seldom take place. At parties every girl feels she must be as well dressed and groomed as the other girls of her social class. Usually her father and mother want her to be and give her no opposition when she keeps up with her friends.

Clothes and Customs

The clothes worn by girls and boys in the cities of the Andean countries are similar to those worn by teen-agers in Canada or the United States, with American movies helping to influence styles. Red, green, blue, and white appear to be the most popular colors. Girls and women usually wear slacks only in the home or around resort areas, and shorts practically never appear anywhere. Men and teen-age boys also refuse to wear shorts, which seem to be reserved for boys not yet in their teens.

In Lima almost nobody wears a hat unless it is part of a uniform, and few white people in the capitals of Ecuador and Bolivia wear them. Away from the largest cities some white people wear hats, as do many mestizos and nearly all Indians other than teen-agers and children. People who wear them may keep them on in ordinary restaurants, libraries, and other public places where Americans usually take them off. In Ecuador and to some extent in Bolivia many people also sit through a movie or dinner, except at a fashionable restaurant, with raincoats and topcoats on even when there is no need for extra warmth. Because so many people go without hats, they give considerable attention to their hair. Women wear their hair long, either done up in permanents, braided, or hanging straight. The ponytail has become popular and to some extent has replaced braided hair among older non-Indian women and even occasionally among Indian girls. All men wear their hair fairly full but never long and stringy down over their ears or collars. Many men have moustaches, but few bother with beards unless they are in the arts or are students.

Wearing one's hat in a public place, such as the municipal library of Iquitos, Peru, is commonplace

So Goes the Day

Some male students take their work much more seriously than most girls do. As a result, they lack girl friends. While most teen-agers date, ambitious students study their lessons, but otherwise their days are much the same as those of other young people. Ordinarily during the school year, which runs from March to December, a school boy gets up about seven in the morning. If time permits, as in Bolivia where classes start about nine and in Peru where they begin at eight thirty, he showers and dresses leisurely. With many Ecuadorian schools opening at eight, the student there must hurry to get ready. In all three countries students swallow a hasty breakfast, often of fruit or fruit juice, untoasted bread, and coffee that is half hot milk. Many Bolivian youngsters prefer hot chocolate to coffee, yet in all these lands boys and girls start drinking coffee and tea almost as soon as they're born. An unusually hungry youngster might breakfast on a fried egg, ham, or jelly sandwich. Bacon is not especially popular.

Schools let out at eleven thirty or noon and are closed for two to three hours. This is the lunch and siesta period, but young people never spend any of it sleeping. Every youngster who can do so goes home for lunch, which will be a big meal if the family can afford it. It starts with soup and a salad. By the father's plate sits a small bell, which the head of the household rings when he wants a maid to clear the plates for one course and bring the next one. This keeps servants from milling in and out needlessly during the meal. (At an ordinary restaurant you can clap your hands for the waiter if you become impatient for him to bring the next course, but in a smart eating place you should wait quietly.) After the opening courses come the meat and vegetables. Beef, mainly steaks and roasts, and chicken appear on tables frequently. A favorite vegetable in Peru is rice, while potatoes are particularly common in Bolivia.

A university student does his math lessons on a park bench in Callao, Peru

143

Some people eat veal and lamb for variety, but pork finds less favor. With Ecuador and Peru being fishing countries, you might expect the people to eat quantities of seafood. Actually, much of the catch is exported, and what is sold locally proves fairly expensive so is none too popular. Food prices in countries of the central Andes run about as they do in the States, with some items costing a bit less.

These countries usually produce less meat than their people eat. As a result, large sums of money must be spent to import meat. In 1968 the Peruvian government tried to cut down import expenses by forbidding shops to sell meat on Mondays and Tuesdays. In a country where refrigerators and freezers are not commonplace, such a restriction did have some effect, though many people made a game of finding ways to avoid observing meatless days. After the meat course a family has dessert. In Peru and Ecuador this will most often be fruit. Bolivians sometimes have cookies, pie, or cake, as they eat more pastries than most Latin Americans. Coffee usually ends the meal. Only for special occasions will a family have wine with either lunch or dinner. For this reason young people are likely to learn to drink away from home rather than in the family circle as they would do in some other South American countries.

Students return to school between two and three in the afternoon and are let out for the day between four and five. Most of the time they go right home from school to have tea. In Peru this is called *lonche,* which sounds like "lunch" but can better be interpreted as "snack." It somewhat resembles breakfast in Peru and Ecuador, but in Bolivia it may be similar to a small lunch and take the place of dinner. Food cannot be digested as easily in high altitudes as near sea level. Bolivians know it is best to do their heavy eating during the day when they are most active rather than in the evening after the day's work has been done. Adults in offices also stop for *lonche* in Peru or a tea break in Bolivia and Ecuador. Tea is often served right in the office in Bolivia, and a company that fails to provide a tea break can be fined. In Peru and Ecuador workers may have tea at their desks but many go out to nearby cafés. Teas can be made from a variety of plants, even from violet blossoms, but ordinary tea is most common.

144

Youngsters taking music lessons or special courses offered at a cultural institute go to these classes after tea. Otherwise the school child should settle down to his homework, which probably amounts to some reading. Whether or not he does it depends on how strict his parents are and how ambitious he is. Casual students use the time to chat with friends, play games, or watch television (except in Bolivia where TV has not yet arrived). In strict homes on weekdays students must leave the television set alone until about eight in the evening. Dinner is served between seven and nine, which is early for Latin America. It may be a fairly big meal but seldom offers as many courses as lunch. Many families omit salad for dinner and serve small portions of meat. Hamburgers and hot dogs are favorite foods for dinner. Bolivians, if they have dinner, have a light dessert instead of pastry. In any of the countries fruits may be served for dessert, though Peruvians often like a sweet, perhaps rice pudding or gelatin. Again, coffee concludes the meal. After dinner a student may turn to his books if he neglected them

Bread, rolls, and big doughnuts come to market in a wheelbarrow. Here a priest looks over the wares. Though Bolivian clerics stick to traditional Catholic robes, European and American missionaries are adopting ordinary dress

earlier, but much of the time the family spends the evening watching television. Small children go to bed between nine and ten, while teenagers follow between eleven and twelve. Since Bolivia has no television, youngsters there go to bed earlier than those in Ecuador and Peru. If the light is good enough, a teen-ager may read something popular before going to sleep.

For the Hungry

You can easily see that food holds great interest for Latin Americans. Except for the poor, who may not have one good meal a day, people seem to be eating much of the time. In Bolivia, in addition to regular meals and afternoon tea, people have a morning snack between ten thirty and eleven. They eat *salteñas,* which are little *empanadas* that contain up to eighteen ingredients and are highly spiced. *Salteñas* are so full of juice a person needs skill to eat one without getting messy. After noon you can't buy one again that day, and everyone would know you were a foreigner if you asked for one in the afternoon or evening. Kids, especially in Peru, love *cochas,* which are types of sugar candies made in large blocks. A candy store owner shoos away the flies and whacks a block with a hammer to break off pieces. He sells a few pieces at a time for a penny or so.

In cooking, people of the central Andes countries use generous quantities of pepper and exotic spices. However, at restaurants frequented by tourists, soups and other dishes are usually mild. Many soups are thick with vegetables—potatoes, corn, carrots, onions—and some contain meat. Corn may still be on the cob, while a piece of meat may be so large that it is necessary to "cut the soup with a knife." Different regions have their different foods and dishes, as do various festival periods. Sausages have become particularly popular in Bolivia. They were introduced originally by the Spanish, but the many Germans who have come to the country have brought in German and Polish sausages. Local people have developed their own variations, using quantities of hot peppers, garlic, oregano, and tumeric. These become so fiery that it takes a true Bolivian to eat them. Potatoes can be made rather special with peanuts. A cook grinds *aji amarillo* (chili pepper) pods and mixes

146

A salesman of fruits and nuts in Callao, Peru, can pedal his stand to any promising location

them with the nuts and a cheese to form a sauce. She heats this and pours it over the potatoes after they have boiled. Hard-boiled eggs and black olives are placed around the dish or can be cut up and sprinkled over it. Olives of the Andes are usually small, mostly pit, and rather bitter.

Inside the Home

Parents sometimes find it difficult to keep youngsters from eating in front of the television set. In the homes of the upper classes each room has its specific function, and food should be eaten in the dining room.

Young people, less troubled by traditions than their parents, find *empanadas* taste just as good in the living room as elsewhere. Mothers, particularly, worry that stains will get on the furniture. Many of the furnishings in Peruvian and Bolivian homes are heavy pieces, such as overstuffed chairs, massive dining tables, big chests of drawers, and the like. In Ecuador light furniture has become popular. Ecuadorians do beautiful woodcraft, and many people feel the wooden furniture can compete with the light, modern tables and chairs for which Denmark receives so much credit. Rugs, produced in Peru and Ecuador, cover the floors. Bolivians probably have fewer rugs, but scatter alpaca-wool mats about here and there to give an attractive touch to a room. Reed and hemp mats serve in poorer homes if anything is used to cover the floors.

People almost always paint their walls. A family may include one local scene among the pictures hung on the walls, and often there will be a few religious paintings. One picture of the Madonna or of Christ hangs in each bedroom when the family is seriously religious, and many homes have a "Last Supper" in the dining room. In a home in Ecuador this "Last Supper" may be molded or sculpted in silver and will be

This Puno mother weaves with one hand while she holds her child with the other. The rug, which will take weeks to finish, will be for sale rather than for her family's use

one of the most expensive treasures in the house. Somewhere in the home, probably in the living room, stands a religious figure. A priest blesses a new house in the countries of the central Andes, and this religious figure receives a sprinkling of holy water during the ceremony. Friends and relatives attend the blessing and afterward help celebrate by drinking champagne where the family can afford it. Practically every home has photographs of the family members. These pictures stand in frames or hang on the walls, and where the household is nonreligious they may be the only pictures used for decorations.

Fun and Games

In addition to school, dating, and home activities, young people find plenty of time to play. Before they reach their teens, boys like to spin tops. A boy winds a string around the top and throws it down on a flat surface with considerable force to give it a fast whirl. Then he slips his fingers under the point and tries to get it into the palm of his hand while it continues to spin. The most adept spinner can toss it into the air from his palm and catch it, still whirling, on the back of his hand. Another favorite toy, especially in Bolivia, is the slingshot. Unfortunately, dogs, cats, song birds, and even people sometimes suffer when a boy feels like getting even with the world. Few young people have dogs and cats as pets but are more likely to have parrots, guinea pigs, and monkeys if they have pets at all. Since dogs and cats serve as rodent catchers more often than as pets, some youngsters have less affection for them than they would have if they owned one themselves.

Quite a few youngsters have bicycles, used mainly for pleasure riding, though boys run errands on their bikes. In Bolivia on May 1 (Labor Day) and July 16 (La Paz Day), boys hold "kiddie-car" races down some of the streets blocked off for the purpose. These events are somewhat like soap-box derbies. A car crew consists of a driver and his "motor," which is another boy. The "motor" rides down the steep places but must hop off and push the car on the level or uphill ones. Peru's Labor Day, which is also May 1, is celebrated with firecrackers, skyrockets, and fire balloons. Fire balloons are made of thin paper covered with attractive or gaudy designs. A wad of cotton or rags

Peace Corps volunteer Joe Grant introduces a bit of North American fun to youngsters of Chimbote, Peru, as he teaches them the fundamentals of baseball

soaked in oil dangles on strings below the mouth of a balloon. When merrymakers light the wad of material, warm smoke and gases rise into the paper bag and lift it high above the trees. People enjoy fireworks towers most of all. On a delicate wooden framework twenty or so feet tall, boys string together in sequence all manner of firecrackers and sparklers. When someone lights the fuses, fiery wheels spin, crackers bang, and clusters bob about.

South Americans love sports. Soccer ranks as the number one athletic activity in Bolivia, Ecuador, and Peru, where it is called *futbol*. Basketball, volleyball, and handball also prove popular, with the first two being games girls enjoy as much as boys. In Peru surfboarding has gained considerable attention, and international tournaments have been held in Peruvian waters. Latin American contests in various sports are often held in Lima because Peru is fairly centrally located. Among South Americans, Peruvians generally excel at tennis. Alex Olmedo, from Arequipa, played on a United States championship tennis team. The most unusual sport of the central Andes is probably bullfighting. Peruvians in particular practice it and invite fighters from other countries to their arenas. These have been built mainly in the lowlands. The great fighters, who are mostly from Spain and Mexico, don't want to go to high altitudes where they tire quickly and fighting becomes even more dangerous than usual. This helps explain why Bolivia and Ecuador have not become major bullfighting countries like Peru. The best fighters in the world visit Lima, especially during the main season in October. A few Peruvians have become world famous bullfighters, among them Rafael Santa Cruz, a Negro, who went to Spain to fight after winning acclaim at home.

An Aymara child of Bolivia with her pet kid

Looking after Mind, Body, and Soul

When Ecuador, Peru, and Bolivia existed as Spanish colonies, the Catholic Church concerned itself with education and health as well as with religion. The picture changed during the nineteenth century and the first half of the twentieth, though it has not altered as much in Peru as in Bolivia and Ecuador. The Church in Peru continues to be a major force in planning school curriculums and, to some extent, health services. While the impact of the Catholic Church was being weakened, Protestant mission groups came into the area to exert some influence on education, health, and, to a degree, religion. People in all these fields say many more changes are needed. It will not matter whether they are made by religious groups or secular ones, but they should be made.

Overcrowding

More public school buildings must be built rapidly to meet the needs of growing and shifting populations. In all three countries some schools are so overcrowded that students must attend in shifts. In many areas there is a morning shift, an afternoon shift, and an evening one, with classes lasting only about half an hour. In general, the poorer people attend the night shifts. Sometimes they work by day and can go at no other time, but often they lack the will to fight for a day shift or the money to bribe whoever makes up the schedules.

Away from the capitals and other large cities teachers may be too scarce to permit shifts. During the first weeks of the school year students crowd into the classrooms until some must sit on windowsills or

A male physical education teacher, on the far side of the net, instructs high school girls in volleyball at the Ecuadorian-North American Cultural Institute in Quito. In a strictly Ecuadorian school, a woman would coach the girls

Schoolgirls in Peru, as in most of the central Andes regions, dress uniformly. Here they enter an office building being used for classes because of the shortage of schools

perhaps the teacher's table. Up to eighty may crowd into a room meant for a third that number. Before long, the high drop-out rate in Latin American schools cuts down the attendance. Indifferent teachers give failing marks to the least promising to discourage them. Eventually the classes contain twenty-five to forty students—still too many, but that's quite usual in South America. These students behave better than many in United States schools. For one thing, respect for adults and authority has been drilled into them from their earliest days. Besides, teachers may be permitted to strike students who get unruly. A minor activity like chewing gum in public schools doesn't come under the heading of misbehaving, so one area of tension between student and teacher is avoided. Youngsters who lack anything else frequently chew string or paper, so they might as well have gum. Teachers call them llamas, since they are always "chewing their cuds."

154

Private Schools

Private schools escape some of the problems faced in the public schools. The private ones can limit the number of students, thus keeping classes to a convenient size, and they can turn away slow or troublesome students if they want to. In parts of Latin America private schools nearly all belong to church groups. Many in the central Andes countries also operate through religious organizations, especially in Peru. To get into a parochial school in Peru, a student must have birth and baptismal certificates. Because their parents cannot provide these necessary papers, many youngsters must attend public schools or seek other types of private institutions. Bolivia and Ecuador have many other types, started by individuals and by industrial firms such as banks and factories. Large mines in Bolivia are expected to supply schools for the children of their employees. In each country private schools have to follow the curriculum planned by that nation's ministry of education. A few may be

Not all the Catholic high schools in Ecuador are as impressive as the Colegio La Salle, in Quito, where basketball is a favorite sport of the priests as well as the students

allowed to introduce a change now and then. In this way they function to a degree as experimental workshops, and changes that seem to be improvements may gradually be fitted into all schools.

Private institutions may be on any level, from prekindergarten schools to universities. Generally the teachers in the private schools make more effort to help youngsters than do instructors in public schools. Much of the time private school teachers are better educated than others. When a person opens a private school of his own, he does so because he feels he can accomplish more with students than if he taught in someone else's school. Quite often he is right. Much of the public school teaching follows manuals. In Bolivia most of these date from about 1948, which means they should have been revised, if not discarded, long ago. Some reform measures were drawn up in 1968, but no definite time was planned for putting the changes into effect. The manual in Bolivia for

Barbara Tetrault sketches a rooster named Fidel for a first grade class. A Peace Corps worker, she teaches art in Guayaquil, Ecuador

covering the entire program for all the elementary grades amounts to only 128 pages. Obviously, a great deal should come from a teacher's imagination. But in public schools more teachers seem concerned with getting their pay than with initiating anything beyond the manual, so students suffer. The man who operates his own private school can go far beyond the manual. The systems in Peru and Ecuador are superior to that in Bolivia, but to some degree they also rely on guides written out for the teachers. Fortunately, their manuals don't date back to the 1940s.

To Be a Teacher

Ordinarily, teachers in Peru must finish the seven years of elementary school, graduate from high school after five years, and attend normal school or a university for four years. But graduates of certain bilingual high schools can teach English in the first four grades of elementary school without any college training. The bilingual schools that the government recognizes exist in Lima, and in them teachers and students use Spanish half the day and English the rest of the time.

A teacher on the elementary level in Ecuador goes to normal school for six years after completing the regular six years of elementary work. This gives him the equivalent of a high school education, but he has received special training in how to be a teacher. To teach in high school he needs to take university work but, oddly enough, not necessarily in how to teach. Most secondary school instructors have educated themselves to be lawyers, doctors, chemists, and the like. They go into the schools to handle the courses having some relation to their specific fields. These teachers, with their practical knowledge, help the high school students of Ecuador to become better educated than students of most other countries in South America. A doctor or accountant generally teaches a few hours a week for fairly good pay. The elementary school teacher, by contrast, teaches all day long every day for a poor wage.

In Bolivia each rural instructor should complete the six years of elementary school and then go to a normal school for two years, while the person teaching in a town or city elementary school should have six

A teacher and his pupils at a rural school on the Bolivian high plateau. The students are taught Spanish in school, but continue to speak Aymara at home; such bilingualism is common among Indian students who have attended school since 1952

years of normal school training. With teachers being scarce in Bolivia, careful checks of a person's qualifications aren't always made. Every teacher is supposed to spend two years in the outlying schools—jungle, mountain, or campo—but many teachers try to avoid this. If they teach in town, they can usually live in a pleasant home, get to work easily by public transportation or in a friend's car, and enjoy some social life after school. The country teacher may have to live in a house that lacks indoor plumbing, walk or ride in a truck for some distance to get to the school, and be satisfied with unsophisticated country pleasures.

To make sure some teachers serve in rural areas, officers associated with the Bolivian ministry of education assign teachers to both rural and urban schools. This creates difficulties. In 1968 the people assigned to high mountain regions outside Potosí rebelled because they said the altitude was too great and the climate too cold. It took weeks to get the schools there open, and the teachers, being in a nasty frame of mind, probably did less than their best. A more humorous situation developed in a section of La Paz. Someone forgot to issue the assignment lists, and teachers didn't know where they were to teach. Generally they showed up at the best and newest schools, so some schools had more instructors than they could use while others had almost none until the lists finally appeared.

On the secondary level, in normal schools, and in universities, Bolivian teachers sign up to teach by the hour. An instructor may sign up for classes in several different schools. If he's ambitious, he can take on a heavy load. This pays best, as his salary depends on the number of hours for which he registers. If he's dishonest, he can sign up for far more hours than he can possibly teach. All teachers, in Peru and Ecuador as well as Bolivia, miss many classes—according to some reports one-fourth to one-half of them. So in Bolivia in a normal school in 1968

All school children of Bolivia are supposed to wear white guardapolvos (dust guards), which are intended to make all youngsters look alike and eliminate discrimination

no one showed alarm when one man signed up to teach twenty-eight hours a day.

Among the Students

Few students or parents get upset by such odd situations. If a student eventually gets a certificate of graduation, he thinks he has been educated. And throughout the central Andes less than half the young people finish school. Youngsters in the rural areas receive poorer schooling than those in towns and cities. They study their lessons under teachers who, much of the time, wish they had jobs in urban communities. Some teachers are in the country because they have angered an administrator in town or have shown strong support for a political party that has lost favor. How can students work up much enthusiasm for their courses when these frustrated teachers seldom show a spark of excitement? Observers from other countries often comment on how docile, how absolutely subdued, many of the rural students are. Some teachers, probably seldom being in a good frame of mind, tolerate no nonsense from their pupils and the students become cowed. No wonder urban schools increase their enrollments at a rate double that of country schools.

Almost every rural school lacks laboratory facilities. Science students learn formulas by heart and memorize an assortment of theories with rarely a chance to perform an experiment. Except in the larger cities,

Peace Corps member Greg Labuza needed a school in which to teach, so he built a small one of bamboo matting in Chimbote, a Peruvian coastal city

students of urban schools have little chance to do any better. Until Peace Corps and Papal Volunteer teachers introduced experimental science into the central Andes, almost no school offered any practical science education. These outside teachers often volunteer to work in rural areas, so they help handfuls of students here and there. Unfortunately, there just aren't enough of them to reach great numbers of country students. UNICEF also helps out. It supplies tools and other equipment, and trains some local teachers to work in the mountains. Through the UNICEF programs boys learn to produce gardens and girls to cook and sew. The students work in groups, similar to 4-H Club projects, so they must be in regions where several other youngsters live. Children in isolated families may be unaware that schools exist.

Country schools are usually elementary schools. For additional education, the student goes to a town or other urban center. When he starts high school, a student may carry up to eighteen courses. This doesn't weigh him down as much as you might think. He meets many of the courses only once or twice a week. Students usually buy their own texts. Books for classes in Spanish seldom cost below $2, and those for English literature may cost as much as $20. Only wealthy families can afford many texts, so most schools manage without them. The teacher has a text and a manual from which he reads lessons that the students copy down. Few schools have libraries to which pupils can go to check anything they miss in class. As a result, a student needs to be good at taking notes or should have a friend who is good at it. Getting educated amounts to a great deal of memorizing of the notes one takes.

Higher Education

Universities generally charge small tuition fees—$10 to $25—but require special assessments for courses that include laboratory work. The Catholic University in Lima introduced a new plan in 1968. It attempted to charge tuition according to what a student's family could afford to pay. Many people agreed this was a move in the right direction. Officials and educators all over South America watched with interest, for governments and other contributors find it increasingly difficult to support the institutions of higher learning. The students of

Crowds gather during the week of enrollment at the Ministry of Education in Lima, Peru

162

the Catholic University launched an immediate protest and threatened to go on strike. To get ahead of them, the school closed its doors and no classes met during April and the first half of May. A study of the new tuition program indicated it had been set up too hastily and probably was rather unfair to many young people. But a bold step had been taken, and others most surely will follow.

University students until recently have studied to be teachers, doctors, or lawyers. The trend in the second half of the 1960s saw young people turning to engineering and other sciences, business administration, and economics. Whatever he studies, every student feels he should be at the top of his profession after he graduates. Consequently, one of the big needs throughout the central Andes today is for people to fill the positions between the unskilled laborers and the university-graduated specialists. A whole scale of technicians, laboratory assistants and the like is needed to close the gap between the bottom and the top.

Most students lean to the left politically, partly because they consider it the clever or daring thing to do and partly because they fear they will be left out of activities if they don't. A few, aware of Russia's advances in many fields under Communism, sincerely believe their countries must try a similar course or be forever underdeveloped. Though they call themselves leftists, students may be anti-Moscow, anti-Peking, and anti-Havana. In Bolivia in 1968 some groups broke with the student-body organization that has long wielded the strongest influence. They claimed it had swung too far left in favoring Peking. Many observers foolishly thought this meant the breakaway groups had swung to right of center. No such thing has happened, and even to hope for it is wishful thinking. Most students stand left of center, but with the mild leftists now openly opposing the radical ones.

Experiments

A student from kindergarten through high school has no say in the courses he studies. In high school he may get a choice between college-preparatory work and vocational-guidance courses, but he has no freedom to pick his own subjects. Until the mid-1960s the university student faced the same restriction. Then Peruvian private universities

163

began experiments in giving students a chance to take elective courses in addition to required ones. As a result, students enjoy their university work more and make greater efforts to excel. They graduate with a fuller education instead of one restricted to a single field. Another improvement fits courses into logical time spans. Previously, every course ran for the full nine months' term. Some deserve no more than three or four months, while others should have a term and a half, and the new system attempts to give each subject the amount of time it merits. Only private universities tried the new system in the beginning, but public institutions of higher learning watched to see what the results would be. Encouraging early reports made it seem likely that all Peruvian universities and probably many in other countries would eventually change.

Help for the Handicapped

Not many years ago, educators in South America felt health problems should be faced by doctors, not by teachers. Any retarded youngster, instructors thought, did not belong in a school. Yet a few dedicated people have worked for about two decades to establish schools for the handicapped, and in the 1960s their efforts finally won wide acclaim. Much of the credit for the change should go to a Bolivian boy who was born without arms or legs and a French-American woman who saved him from neglect. The woman, French-born Ann Wasson, went to Bolivia in 1944 with her American husband who had a wartime assignment there. After World War II they remained in the country to help needy people. One day a mestizo child without arms or legs was discovered where he had been abandoned on the patio of a poor family's home in La Paz. Juan Irigoyen's hands grew directly out of his shoulders, and his feet grew from his trunk. When Mrs. Wasson heard of Juan, she worked to interest New York doctors in helping him. His case was so unusual that it became world famous. The Wassons got Juan to New York, where he in time received artificial arms and legs. He also obtained an education and returned to Bolivia as a self-supporting member of society. The publicity connected with Juan Irigoyen's case has done much to interest other people throughout Latin America in aiding the handicapped.

164

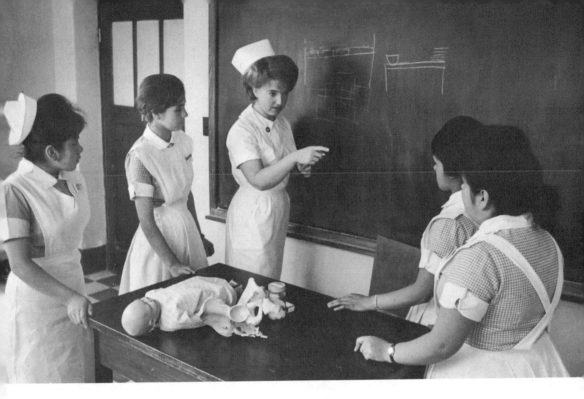

Gayle Standring, a volunteer nurse for the Peace Corps, helps train student nurses in a La Paz, Bolivia, hospital

Medicine for Body and Soul

Other changes must come. The poor people need to be educated to respect human life. For every Juan Irigoyen abandoned where he will be found, countless numbers of handicapped Indian and mestizo babies are left in deserted gullies of the altiplano. Even the normal baby in some mountain districts has less than a 50–50 chance of survival. In remote sections of Bolivia and probably of all three countries seven out of ten infants die, and even in the largest cities the death rate may be three or four out of ten. Ignorant midwives need to be replaced by trained ones, nurses, or doctors. Yet where decent medical facilities are available, many women follow age-old superstitious practices and avoid contact with the nurses and doctors who could help them. An expectant mother often avoids a hospital because she knows of the crowded conditions and fears she will have to share a bed with another

To help combat the problem of malnutrition, Martha Iwaski runs a breakfast program for 4,000 school children in Chimbote, Peru

expectant mother. Nurses who seldom change their uniforms, scrub their hands, or perform their duties quickly and well make many people look down on the profession. People fear all nurses because they hear about this type instead of the careful, competent ones.

Since medicine is one of the favored fields of study in the central Andes, doctors should be plentiful. They are not. Too many students fail to graduate, and of those who do, some go to other lands where they can make more money. Nearly all of those who stay home want to practice where they can make a fortune. In a poor community a doctor may charge a patient only about $1 for a visit, but in wealthy sections of large cities doctors get $10 for the same amount of service. Some communities therefore have an abundance of doctors while others have almost none. The main problems faced by doctors include malnutrition, tuberculosis, and internal parasites. Many youngsters look

166

chubby and healthy when in reality they are merely bloated and infested with worms. Malaria sometimes crops up, but pesticides have pretty well wiped out the mosquitoes that transmit it. Kala-azar, which produces fever and anemia, also causes trouble along the coasts of Peru and Ecuador, but insecticides generally control the sandflies responsible for it. Yellow fever, smallpox, plague, and typhus, which once reached epidemic proportions in the countries of the central Andes, have all been brought under control. Few people seem to think of alcoholism as a medical problem. Heavy drinking is an accepted social custom, and reportedly Ecuadorians and Bolivians consume more alcoholic beverages per capita than the peoples of any other Latin American nation.

Poor hospital conditions exist in all three countries, especially away from the large cities. In sections of Bolivia conditions are so bad that a person takes it for granted doctors have given him up to die if they

These Indians moved the contents of their home outside so the interior could be checked and sprayed for disease-carrying insects

put him in a hospital. His friends and relatives dress in black when they come to visit him. Any Bolivian who can afford it goes to Chile, Argentina, or the United States to have an operation. When a person cannot avoid going to a hospital, particularly in Bolivia, he may take his own nightgown and bedding. This assures him not only that he will have these things but that they will be clean. If prescription medicines fit his case, he may buy them ahead of time and take them to the hospital also. In Bolivia, hospitals give a cool welcome to a patient who comes in under social security benefits. The government seldom has the money to pay a man's bill even though he has regularly been giving up 7½ per cent of his salary to the social security program, and his employer has been paying up to 33 per cent for him besides. The governments of Peru and Ecuador manage to meet many of their welfare obligations, so a social security patient in those countries usually does not suffer the neglect that he might in Bolivia.

Few of the Indians on the altiplano know what a hospital is. If they do know, they distrust such an institution and want no dealings with it. They put their faith in potions, incantations, and omens. When a rare doctor turns his back on a profitable city practice to try to help the people on the campo, he encounters frustration more often than achievement. If he perseveres and studies the people, he finally learns to use a little trickery along with his pills and vaccinations. He borrows a chant from a witch doctor or makes up an incantation of his own and mumbles this while jabbing a patient with a needle or pouring medicine down a boy's throat. He may tell a woman to bury a few hairs from her left eyebrow under a rock on a moonless night in addition to taking the tablets he gives her. Word spreads that he differs from most doctors and *sanitarios* (health workers), and gradually the Indians develop faith in him.

Itinerate priests have traveled the altiplano since the days of the conquistadors, so they receive more trust than doctors. Originally the ministers went on foot. Later they journeyed by burro, and today they hitchhike or drive some sort of old vehicle of their own. A truck driver never passes a priest who hails a ride. At isolated farms and in small villages these priests bless houses, perform weddings, baptize babies, and tend to other religious duties. They may have to sleep in icy barns or lice-infested huts, but they continue their rounds year after year until their health breaks down. They are among the most dedicated religious men of the central Andes.

In the twentieth century various Protestant groups have carried their work into western South America. Methodists and Baptists conduct schools and operate health clinics, as do other groups. Even in the second half of the twentieth century some have been massacred by the wild jungle tribes they hoped to Christianize. When this has happened, the churches to which they belonged have made plans to try again. Their schools and clinics receive more visitors than their pews, which is what happens all over the world. Everyone agrees they take burdens off governments unable to cope with all the educational and health problems in a region where problems are plentiful.

Legends or Miracles?

No one can say whether or not an Indian ever entirely accepts Christianity. A *campesino* may live as a believer for most of his life, yet suddenly call on some strange spirit when faced with an unexpected

Aymara Indians observe holy days at Las Peñas. A Maryknoll mission located here serves a community of many square miles; the mission's transmitter broadcasts basic education to outlying areas equipped with receivers

emergency. Some Indians who live Christian lives openly retain the hope that Eqeqo (Ekeko) will reward them. Eqeqo resembles a pagan Santa Claus and comes from ancient Aymara beliefs. This spirit has a special day, January 24. On that day salesmen set up stalls and offer all manner of little models—furniture, cars, food, houses, burros, oxen, plows, and the like. Legend says Eqeqo will bring you the real thing if you buy one of these small-scale items before noon on the 24th of January. Some men have been so sure of getting a car or a house that they have hired a driver or a maid in order to be ready. Later, they have had to let these servants go when the wished-for possession never turned up. And it's not just Indians who buy the models. Mestizos and white people, perhaps more secretly, also buy them, just as they buy lottery tickets. Many a serious Christian prayer has been said over a lottery ticket.

Some Indians see little difference between belief in Eqeqo and in the many Christian miracles (most of which are not recognized by the Church) that they are told have taken place in the central Andes. For instance, a rather involved miracle reportedly took place about four hundred years ago at Peñas, a small Bolivian village high in the mountains. A Negro slave supposedly discovered a small oven-shaped cave in which an image of the Virgin of the Nativity lit up the surrounding rocks. He resolved never to leave her, and made his home in a large animal den nearby. The light from her face drove all the witch doctors from the place, and the people who saw this began to worship her. They carried the image to a church nearby, but during the night it returned to the grotto—no one knew how. Again they took her to the church. This time they guarded the building, yet the image returned to its place in the side of the mountain. After several unsuccessful attempts to install it in the church, the mothers of the area prayed to the Virgin to remain and bring an end to the sinful ways of the young men thereabouts. This time, for a week, the Virgin remained, so frightening the young men that they did improve their behavior. After a week the Virgin mysteriously returned to the grotto. In the meantime, the slave, thinking she had deserted him, had died of sorrow. The people took the image to the church once more and buried the Negro beside her altar. Thereafter she remained in the church.

A few years later on the Virgin's feast day, September 8, a crippled woman of La Paz set out to visit the grotto in hopes of receiving some relief from her pains. After many days the women could hardly continue, even on hands and knees, and she feared she might have to give up. But her faith told her to keep going. At last she came to a river. There was no way for her to cross, and in despair she fainted. The sound of hooves brought her to her senses. She looked up to discover a charging bull almost ready to trample her underfoot. Before she could move, it lowered its head and lifted her gently on its massive horns. It swam across the river to carry her to the church of the Virgin. There she crawled inside, felt a shudder pass through her body, and stood up to walk and run about without any further aid of the sticks she had carried as crutches. Reportedly, some of Bolivia's most exciting bullfights have taken place in this area, and it is said that on September 8 the bulls come down to the village of their own accord, ready for the fights.

If the legend involved the lowlands of Peru or if Bolivia were more of a bullfighting country, the Indians might find the story easier to believe. As it is, no one really knows whether they believe it or not. Some claim to, others just shrug, but Indians are noted for telling a man what he wants to hear. If they think he wants them to believe the legend, they'll say they believe it. But they also ask why he won't believe in some of their traditional stories. If the Indian is to be made to truly believe in Christianity, he must be educated. If he is to be made to see the value of sanitation and other health measures, he must be educated. Time and again, anyone hoping to help the poor of the central Andes comes back to this one basic fact—education for everybody is of prime importance and no change, revolution, or prayer will be fully effective without it.

The Arts

The ancient Incas enjoyed music, theater, and artistic handcrafts. When white men arrived in the central Andes, they imposed their culture on the Indians until few truly native art forms remain. The Indians themselves show slight interest in reviving them, and most efforts along these lines are made by a few dedicated people of European descent. The art forms that have the best chance of survival seem to be those with strong commercial possibilities, and alien flourishes have been added to old styles to make them more "salable." This caused "purists" to complain when Lima held its first Labor Day music fiesta on May 1, 1968.

The fiesta did serve a worthwhile purpose. Many laborers around Lima are Indian and mestizo people who have come from the sierra, but unless a man can afford to fly, transportation facilities generally are too poor to allow him to go far in a short time. So the fiesta, held in Lima's bullring, provided hours of music and dance of particular interest to people who could not get away for the holiday. Time and again modern touches kept the musical presentations from being authentic. For instance, a *huayño* is supposed to be a plaintive song. It originated among the Incas of the altiplano and enjoys popularity in all three countries of the central Andes. A particularly successful modern *huayño* is "Sombrero de Sao," or "Hat of Straw."

> To this girl, for her birthday
> I will give a hat of straw
> So that she covers herself and me as well
> When I kiss her under the tree.

Oruro, Bolivia, hosts a lavish Mardi Gras festival each year which is a popular tourist attraction. Participants spend great amounts of time and money in preparing the exotic costumes

173

If her mother catches me in the doorway,
I will greet her with the hat.

"Listen, Madam," I will say,
"Good afternoon, how are you?"

"Listen, lazy good-for-nothing wastrel,
What do you want?"

"Your daughter, Lady Ejta, who else?"
"Do you think to support her with songs?"
"Not with songs, Madam, with this heart."

Obviously, this huayño has comic elements as well as plaintive ones. And since comic elements are better received, commercial touches increase and traditional forms become diluted until they cannot be considered genuine.

Most of the people at the fiesta enjoyed themselves, however. As during a bullfight, the sunny side of the ring cost less than the shady side, and it held a capacity crowd. The spectators fashioned sun hats for themselves out of folded newspaper or bought ready-made ones from vendors. Salesmen also sold ice cream, cool drinks, peanuts, and again as if at a bullfight, souvenirs in the shape of bulls and fighters. A particularly interesting instrument played several times during the afternoon and evening resembled a bugle produced from a curved ram's horn. It made a blaring sound and offered a limited number of notes. A duet of these instruments proved rather nerve-shattering to people who have never heard them before.

Besides the *huayño,* other traditional music forms of the central Andes are the *cueca,* the *taquirari,* and the *bailecito.* A *taquirari* resembles a *huayño* but may be even more lively. The *bailecito,* which is primarily a dance, shows a relationship to the Virginia reel. The *cueca,* the national dance of Bolivia, involves the pursuit of a girl by a boy. All these forms, not just the *cueca* and *bailecito,* can be accompanied by dances. Much of the music of Latin America is romantic, and that of Bolivia proves especially so. This can be seen in the popular *cueca Palomita,* or "Little Dove," from Bolivia's region bordering on Argentina.

You are my little dove
That woke me up
Making my window happy
In the morning, oh yes,
Making my window happy
In the morning, oh yes.

You are my love; happy love
Give me a lifetime in the spring, oh yes.
You are the little dove
Whom I saw, happy, going by
With your pretty face,
Crossing the river Guadalquivir.

Indian farmers playing instruments called quenas *and wearing colorful decorations over their shoulders pay tribute to the patron saint of agriculture on the altiplano*

Folklore Night Clubs

A recent development in La Paz is the *Peña Folklorica*—a combination coffeehouse and wineshop offering shows of fairly authentic folk singing and a little folk dancing as evening entertainments. Three such houses—Naira, Pacha Mama, and Kor Thiki—attract enthusiastic audiences. At one of these you might still hear Bolivia's national instrument, the *charango*. The *charango* resembles a guitar, sounds rather like a banjo, and is made from an armadillo shell. With the guitar being the most common instrument throughout the countries of the central Andes today, you seldom get a chance to hear a *charango* or other instruments from the past. The *quena,* however, remains popular. It is an end-blown flute that resembles a recorder, and Indians play it on festival days.

Many Go; A Few Remain

As in the rest of Latin America, men who win fame in the central Andes often leave the region to live where they can receive more attention or money, especially in Argentina, Mexico, the United States, Great Britain, and Germany. Bolivia's most famous musician, the violinist Jaime Laredo Unzueto, lives in the United States and performs there and in Europe. So does the Bolivian pianist Walter Ponce and the Peruvian pianist Lolo Odiaga. These artists perform standard compositions rather than anything of the Andes. As soon as she gained recognition as a singer with a remarkable range and vocal power, Ima Sumac left Peru for the United States. A local legend says her unusual abilities came from the powerful lungs she developed while chasing her father's goats about the mountains. Carlos Valderrama, one of Peru's most famous musicians of recent times, discovered her and provided much of her training. He was an exception to the rule of leaving home. Though he traveled widely, he spent much of his life in Peru.

Another man who has remained in the central Andes, Rudolfo Holzmann, ranks among Peru's leading composers. He has saved some Peruvian folk themes from extinction, using them in his *Pequeña Suite Peruana,* or "Little Peruvian Suite," and *Concerto para la Ciudad Blanca,* or "Concerto for the White City," which is Arequipa. Holzmann, a German by birth, was the first Peruvian to record music composed by today's descendants of the Incas and to help them get compositions published.

More famous than Holzmann, Enrique Iturriaga stands as Peru's greatest living composer. Like other outstanding musicians, such as Francisco Pulgar and Enrique Pinilla, his orchestral and chamber music is international rather than regional in style.

In Ecuador, Patricia Aulestai uses folk themes for ballets. She conducts one of the two ballet groups in the country, and hers is the main school of native dancing. The most famous dance performed by her troupe is *San Juanito,* which was adapted from an Indian romance. Based on Inca origins, it also shows Spanish influences. She has her headquarters in Quito.

Culture Capitals

Without exception, the capital cities are the main cultural centers. Though other communities have music groups that appear and disappear, theaters that come and go, and occasional art exhibits, every serious artist and performer makes plans to get to the capital of his country. When ballet companies, highly popular in the central Andes, come to South America, they generally remain in the capitals. So do touring instrumental groups and theater companies. They want to be

On hot days an American Papal Volunteer, Patricia Reagan, teaches in an open court of the Peruvian-North American Cultural Institute branch in Arequipa

177

sure of making money. However, when a foreign government, such as that of the United States, sends a cultural group on a goodwill tour, it may visit several cities in each country in addition to the capital. Most universities have at least small cultural groups, but these schools don't sponsor such activities on a large scale. In each of these three countries cultural institutes exist that are sponsored jointly by the national government and the United States. These take some responsibility for presenting traveling cultural groups.

No capital of the central Andes has a "Broadway." Much of the professional theater comes from Argentina, Chile, North America, and Europe, while only half a dozen local groups manage to survive from year to year. Actors in Peru generally fare better than those in Ecuador and Bolivia, and a few performers have devoted followings. Television in Peru and Ecuador gives actors of those countries a chance to increase their fame. Yet some performers consider TV beneath them and will not act before the cameras. These are usually the same performers who will not go outside the capital cities to take part in shows. Most people who have won recognition in the theater show little interest in providing young people with entertainment. Perhaps the outstanding exception is Sara Joffré in Lima. She directs one of the city's most active theater groups, presenting plays for both adults and children. She writes many short plays for young people and is the only dramatist in the central Andes writing regularly for a children's theater.

Playwrights and Plays

Joffré has not achieved the fame of Sebastian Salazar Bondy, considered Peru's greatest playwright until he died in the mid-1960s. Salazar wrote both comedies and dramas in which he considered the troubles of the lower classes. He called himself the "painter of the sad middle class," but many of his works concentrated on the poor, especially of Peru's coastal region. A typical Salazar play is *Ifigenia en el Mercado* ("Iphigenia in the Market"), which is about a girl from the coast who goes to Lima and finds herself faced with overpowering problems.

Other noteworthy Peruvian dramatists are Enrique Solari Swayne, writing in a realistic vein; Juan Rivera Saavedra, Peru's leading playwright of the absurd; and Juan Rios, creator of poetic plays. With even less theater in Bolivia and Ecuador than in Peru, writers of those countries have little chance to establish themselves as dramatists. Popular in Ecuador are American musicals, with the less complicated ones like *The Music Man* receiving frequent productions.

Especially in Bolivia, a writer is a poet first and turns to novels or plays as an additional form of expression.

The Book World

One of the greatest novels from the central Andes countries originated in Ecuador. Calling it *Huasipungo,* Jorge Icaza wrote it to present problems of modern-day Indians. The title is a word that means a small patch of land an Indian works but doesn't own, which means he must share the produce from it with a landlord. The English translation goes by the title *The Villagers,* which fails to convey the misfortune inherent in the original.

One of Bolivia's most famous authors was Franz Tamayo. A prize for literature is given in his name, and one of its outstanding winners has

At a shoeshine and comic book stand in Ambato, Ecuador, youths rent comics which they must pay for in advance and read on the premises

been Sergio Suarez Figueroa, who died early in 1968. Of its younger writers, Bolivia looks hopefully to Guido Calavi Abaroa, who published a novel, poetry, and plays while still a university student.

In publishing, Peru resembles the United States more than Bolivia and Ecuador do. And this has become true in Peru only since World War II. Until recent times an author generally paid the costs of having his books published, but today the better publishing houses take care of the expenses. Peruvian publishers once waited for authors to come to them, but as they make more money they go in search of authors. They read stories and poetry in local magazines and papers in hopes of discovering talent. Ecuadorian and Bolivian authors still usually help with the costs and have to seek out the publishers.

Few people endeavor to make a living writing for children. Oscar Alfaro and Mercedes Anaya de Urquidy of Bolivia are popular with young readers, as are Carlota de Nuñez and Maria Telleria in Peru.

Magazines

Young people have few magazines to choose from. What there are come into the central Andes from Argentina, Mexico, Chile, and the United States. You see great numbers of Spanish-language comic books, with Walt Disney comics having widespread popularity. *Batman* and *Superman* comics also attract many readers. In Bolivia there are shops —sometimes bookstores, sometimes barbershops—and in Ecuador there are shoeshine stands that rent comic books. At the Bolivian shops a boy brings in a comic and then borrows one for about a fourth of what it would cost new. When he brings it back, he can take another on the same basis. At an Ecuadorian shoeshine stand the reader pays less but must do his reading on the premises and does not have to bring in a comic of his own to start with. Reading on the premises is the accepted practice throughout the central Andes. The only adult libraries to loan out books are those established in the cultural institutes sponsored jointly by the national governments and the United States.

For adults a wider selection of magazines exists. Pictorial, cultural, political, and news magazines can be found in all three countries. Many of these originate in the States or are based on North American periodicals such as *Life, Time, Newsweek, Popular Mechanics, Playboy, Mad,* and *Mr. America. Vision* is produced in the United States especially for sale in Latin America. Almost all magazines available in Bolivia originate outside the country. Local publications are started from time to time but always have a short life. Major Ecuadorian magazines include *Estadio* for sports and *La Bunga,* which is devoted largely to political satire. Leading Peruvian magazines include *Caretas,* on the order of *Look* or *Life,* and *Oiga,* on the order of *Newsweek* or *Time. Amaru* stands out in Peru as an important cultural magazine. It is published by the University of Engineering in Lima. Even its most eager supporters can't help but remember that in the past other magazines of the arts have had brief popularity.

Newspapers

Newspapers generally resemble those of the United States, not only in appearance but in content. They carry comic strips, horoscopes, crossword puzzles, satiric cartoons (except in Bolivia, where people don't seem to possess a cartoon sense), household hints, sports, and feature columns as well as news. Peru's *Prescencia* has particularly good photo reproduction, though usually newspapers of the central Andes run fewer pictures than North American papers. *Prescencia* must answer to the Catholic Church, but other papers, like *El Diario* in Peru and *La Prensa* in Bolivia, enjoy independence. Modernization of newspapers, especially in Bolivia, has come in recent years. Until the mid-1960s *El Comercio* of La Paz carried advertisements on the front page.

Television

Television offers considerable news coverage. Most locally produced shows are journalistic in content and presentation, with the largest number of music, theatrical, and variety productions coming in from other countries. Television stars of the United States have good followings in Ecuador and Peru. Even humorous programs that get panned in North America go over well in the central Andes. Comedy shows, such as *I Love Lucy* and *The Dick Van Dyke Show,* may have Spanish dubbed in. For musical and variety shows a Spanish narrator usually explains what is going on as the program progresses. Private owners generally control television. They belong to the upper class, as do newspaper and magazine owners, so they almost always have the same point of view as the politicians and churchmen and therefore escape censorship. Even so, everything shown on television in Peru must first meet the approval of the government and the Church. In Peru the government sponsors educational programs to help working people learn to read and write.

This would indicate that even the poor have TV, and if at all possible they do. In Ecuador as well as in Peru a family may go without well-rounded meals in order to own a set. To help pay for it, the owners charge the neighbors to come in and watch. The shows start in the afternoon and run until about midnight.

Radio stations also operate fewer hours than those in the United States. Since television has come to the central Andes, radio stations concentrate heavily on music programs. In Bolivia, where there is no television as yet, comedy and journalistic radio programs remain popular. They will probably die out when the country starts a TV network, which it hopes to do before the mid-1970s. Arrangements for a Spanish company to introduce television into Bolivia are even now underway, and a priest, who had been active in radio, has been sent to the United States to learn all he can about the television industry.

Motion Pictures

All three countries of the central Andes have plans for building motion-picture industries. Bolivia's first feature-length movie came out in 1968 and attracted large crowds. Called *Mina Alaska,* it took place in part around a famous mine named the Alaska. Enough episodes occurred in other regions to allow it to cover most of the different sections of the country, so the film had some likeness to a travelogue. Produced in color, it was praised for "fairly good" photography, and a chase through the mine offered excellent suspense; most critics accepted it as a promising first effort. Because all materials for filmmaking, in Ecuador and Peru as well as in Bolivia, must be shipped in, the making of pictures proves costly, and advances will come slowly. To keep down its expenses, Ecuador has started motion-picture production in association with Mexican companies. Some outstanding Mexican actors have performed in the first films produced, which in general seem designed to attract tourists to Ecuador. The beautiful local landscape serves as a background for imitation James Bond pictures.

Produced in 1966, *En el Cielo No Hay Estrellas* ("There Are No Stars in the Sky") is one of Peru's efforts to get a foothold in the film industry. It won a prize at a film festival in Russia, though some doubting Thomases wonder if this was an effort on Russia's part to win more favor among Peruvians. The film stirred up so much interest among Peru's young people that the director, Armando Robles Godoy, opened an academy to teach the making of films.

Painting and Painters

In painting, as in much else, Peru leads the countries of the central Andes. Its artists have introduced trends that have influenced painters in both Bolivia and Ecuador. Near the beginning of the twentieth cen-

"Retrato de la Señora Luisa de Mesones" by Daniel Hernandez, and "Marcha del Inca" by Teófilo del Castillo

"Retrato de Enrique Camino Brent" by José Sabogal, and "Composicion" by Ricardo Grau

tury Daniel Hernandez started the academic trend in Peru. He launched the National School of Painting about the time World War I ended and produced rather prettified subjects, such as women posed with flowers. At about the same time Teófilo del Castillo introduced impressionism in Peru, while drawing on history for his subject matter. In rebellion against the academic style and influenced by Mexican artists, José Sabogal started the indigenistic movement. He concentrated on truly Peruvian subjects—landscapes, Indians, the coast—and used colors in most unconventional ways. He was widely imitated in the 1920s and 1930s, but his influence gave way in the 1940s to European expressionism, employed particularly by Ricardo Grau. In 1949 the first abstract exhibition in Peru took place. It created a sensation, and most young painters became abstractionists, with Fernando Szyszlo winning top honors. Today most art follows leading United States and European styles, with abstract works dominating.

184

Reportedly the New World's first art school developed in Quito in 1552 under the leadership of two Flemish friars, Jodoko Ricke and Pedro Gosseal. A famous seventeenth century Ecuadorian artist, Miguel de Santiago, was of Indian and Spanish descent. His most famous painting is "Christ in Agony." Legend says he could not get his model to show sufficient suffering. Suddenly the artist plunged a dagger into the model's chest and was rewarded with a look of real agony that enabled him to complete the picture. It makes a fine story but seems rather unlikely. Among native artists, Manuel Chili became highly skilled in the 1700s. A Quito Indian, he worked under the name Caspicara. Ecuador's best-known artist today has Indian blood and proudly admits it. In fact, Osvaldo Guayasamín (whose name means "White Bird Flying") likes to think of himself as an Indian, but he is actually a

A mural by Ecuador's most famous artist, Osvaldo Guayasamín, decorates one end of the Law Building at Central University in Quito

mestizo. For subject matter, modern man and his problems interest Guayasamín, who has developed an individual abstract style while most Ecuadorians imitate other men. Politically he leans far left, but his pictures avoid being mere propaganda pieces.

Most of Bolivia's outstanding artists have moved to other countries. Marina Nuñez del Prado, probably the country's best sculptress, has gone to Mexico, as has Lorgio Vaca, while Maria Luisa Pacheco lives in New York. Although Luis Zilveti still lives in La Paz, he is quite young for a successful artist and no one expects him to remain at home. Like Zilveti, most aspiring artists live in the capital of their country once they decide to work seriously. A typical artist will stay with relatives and strive for an exhibition in one of the local galleries as soon as he has fifteen to twenty canvases or sculptures to show. Next he hopes to be shown in another Latin American country, especially Chile, Argentina, or Mexico (Bolivians and Ecuadorians dream of being exhibited in Peru). His best chance is to be shown at a university. Success gives him prestige at home and helps to get him exhibited at a university in the United States. This, in turn, should lead to his being presented at the Pan American Union in Washington, D. C., a most important step toward having works purchased by art museums anywhere in the world. It is also of importance in winning a scholarship or grant to study

A stained glass window honors Tomás Frias, one-time president of Bolivia for whom the university in Potosí is named

186

At the Oruro Mardi Gras, costumed participants hope to win prizes as they parade before judges in front of a temple of the city

abroad, and that frequently proves to be the reason for moving to another country. During his struggle for success, an artist needs money, for he usually must pay to ship his paintings to exhibits. Unless his family is quite wealthy, he must teach or take commercial commissions of various sorts to tide him over.

Mardi Gras

At festival times many people use their creative abilities to make costumes and elaborate masks. For Mardi Gras in Bolivia particularly, they devote weeks to getting ready and sometimes spend as much money as they make in two or three months. The most lavish Mardi Gras festival occurs in Oruro. Prizes go to the finest costumes, but only a few people can win. Dozens of families suffer for weeks because money that could have been spent for food went into preparations for the festival. Some of the costumes are genuine works of art, and those that win prizes may be preserved in local museums.

187

Economic Problems

On doors of the Economics Building of Central University in Quito's new and handsome University City carved panels show what should be sources of Ecuador's revenues but are sometimes sources of economic difficulty. The top section, with a plane, ship, and train, indicates that transportation is important. And it is, for lack of transportation facilities holds all the countries of the central Andes back. To build roads and railroads up and down high mountains costs millions of dollars, even in countries where laborers earn less than fifty cents an hour. And most ships and planes of western South America are small and aged, hardly capable of competing with the modern giants of other lands.

From Roads to Traffic Cops

One major road enters Ecuador from Colombia, crosses Ecuadorian mountains to enter Peru, follows Peru's level coast, and continues south into Chile. This is the Pan-American Highway. At Arequipa a branch of the road climbs the Peruvian and Bolivian Andes to make its way to La Paz and south into Argentina. Although much of its route uses older roads (even the ancient Inca route in Ecuador), many of these could be traveled only in the dry season before the all-weather highway reached completion. A few other hard-surfaced road systems connect major cities. Trucks make up much of the traffic on the highways. Pickups and small stock trucks predominate, though now and then you see a large oil transport. Japanese-made Toyotas are popular because they are cheaper than vehicles from the United States, but they wear out faster than American trucks in the mountains and deserts.

One economic problem of the Peruvian Andes is land irrigation. Peace Corps volunteer Mike Manetsch helps the villagers of Cuyochico construct a canal across the face of a mountain to water many acres of now unfarmed land

189

Although La Paz, Bolivia, has red and green traffic lights, policemen such as the officer in the little white box on the side of the building, at right, usually operate them by hand. Peru and Ecuador have more automatic traffic lights

A car or truck costs more than twice what it would in the country where it's made, so you seldom find a two-vehicle family. The family that needs a truck goes without a passenger car and uses the truck for pleasure riding as well as all other purposes. Installment-plan buying has become popular in Ecuador, which explains why you see more new vehicles there than in Peru and Bolivia. Catholic Indians and mestizos want their trucks blessed. While a priest says the proper words and sprinkles holy water on a vehicle, friends of the owner shower it with flower petals, decorate it with colored streamers, splash beer over it, and bombard it with noisy but harmless firecrackers.

In Ecuador a boy or girl can get a driver's permit at age sixteen and a regular license at twenty-one, while a Bolivian youngster gets a license at sixteen and a Peruvian teen-ager at eighteen. In all three countries, if parents know the right officials or willingly hand out a bit of money, their youngsters can obtain permits between twelve and fourteen. In theory, at least, a driver must pass a written and a practical test to get a license. Once he has a license, a man tries to get a job as a bus or taxi driver if he finds no other work. Most taxis and many buses belong to private owners. The owners join a *collectivo,* a controlling organization that sets the fares and, in connection with city officials, plans bus routes. If a man has sons who drive, he may buy two or three cabs, as finances allow, and use the boys as drivers. Otherwise, he generally settles for one taxi, as it is difficult to find drivers who can be trusted to turn in honest accounts. Even a close relative other than a son may pocket some change instead of being completely honest. City buses are often in private hands, and the owner drives while his ten-to-fourteen-year-old son collects fares. Larger buses that run between major cities belong to companies.

Large cities have traffic lights to control the flow of vehicles. In Peru and Ecuador these usually work automatically, but in many cities of Bolivia, including the capital, a traffic officer works them by pushing buttons. Frequently, in all three countries, policemen stand at busy intersections to be sure drivers obey the lights. Particularly in Ecuador a patrolman stops any driver who "cheats" a bit. The driver, to avoid getting a ticket, offers to make a little payment (perhaps fifty cents) right then and would be utterly astounded if his offer were refused. An Ecuadorian policeman's income amounts to about $30 a month, on which he cannot possibly raise a family. Government officials take it for granted he will add to his salary, and his actions are really part of an accepted system.

Railways and Waterways

Ecuador has one major rail line, from Quito to Guayaquil, which has a spur to the important inland city Riobamba. Quito lacks the industries of the coastal region, so many goods reach it by way of this railroad. One other line connects Quito to the coast, at San Lorenzo, just below the Colombian border. Many imported goods come down this line to the capital. Otherwise, Ecuador's rail lines run short distances from small ports to towns and large haciendas of the coastal strip.

Bolivia has relatively poor rail service. The main track connects La Paz with Cochabamba, though there are lines between a few of the other large cities. Some of these wind about so much they can hardly accommodate regular trains. For instance, between Potosí and Sucre buses on train wheels, called *autocarriles,* rather than trains carry passengers over a track that probably doesn't have one straight mile. If you admire the gorgeous scenery instead of looking down the cliffs, you will find the ride interesting. You pass through country that might be in a national park—with eroded rock formations, deep valleys, rugged cliffs, here and there green and yellow fields, and soils in reds, yellows, browns, and even green. One of the few places in the central Andes more exciting is Bolivia's Yungas region southwest of La Paz. Here terrifying precipices drop into deep, heavily wooded, and practically unpopulated valleys.

Peru has 2,000 miles of railroad tracks, more than either Bolivia (1,500) or Ecuador (800). But Peru possesses a transportation system that carries far more commerce than either its rail lines or highways. The Amazon River and its tributaries connect the country with the Atlantic Ocean and make it possible for freighters to reach Iquitos and Pucallpa. Goods can be shipped more cheaply over the 2,500 miles of the Amazon between Iquitos and the Atlantic than they can over the 850 miles of highway between Pucallpa and Lima. Bolivia does some shipping down the Paraguay and Pilcomayo rivers, but when she lost part of the Chaco region to Paraguay, she was cut off from the most navigable sections of these waterways. Ecuador, having been separated from the Amazon by Peru, relies to some extent on her coastal rivers for transporting products. The Guayas serves especially for carrying lumber, in great log rafts, and bananas to Guayaquil for export.

Air Services

Until better nagivation systems are installed, airlines of the central Andes will carry on small-scale operations. If the weather proves at all unsuitable, planes remain on the ground. Bolivia, particularly, is handicapped. Most Bolivian airports have no navigation instruments at all, and pilots fly from town to town by noting landmarks, such as high

The autocarriles *of Bolivia are trucks on train wheels. These take on passengers in the depot at Potosí and run down the mountains to Sucre*

mountains, roads, and rivers. If it is cloudy weather, making such guide-posts difficult to see, planes stay out of the air. Despite such drawbacks, numbers of towns and even some villages as well as all cities of the central Andes have airports. These may be only level fields, from which cows and sheep must be chased when a plane arrives, but without them countless numbers of settlements would have little contact with other communities. Telegraph wires connect only major cities as a rule, while telephones are scarce outside the large population centers.

Communications

Even in capital cities telephones cannot be taken for granted. People wait years to get phones and find them expensive. Lack of wires to carry messages causes the trouble. There may be instruments to install in homes and business offices, but what good are they with telephone wires already overloaded? A large company having numerous offices in one building often installs its own internal telephone system, which operates on large dry-cell batteries. To attract the switchboard operator, you turn a crank by hand. If you are staying at a hotel, you may be charged for receiving incoming calls as well as for making calls. Phone booths are rare. People who eat regularly at a restaurant have no qualms about asking to use the business phone, if the establishment has one, to make personal calls. In Bolivia if a revolution or riots are expected, the American Embassy calls all Americans who have phones and warns them to stay home. This is possible because so few people have phones. In all of La Paz, with its population of half a million and suburbs of equal size, only a few thousand phones exist. When a person manages to get a phone, he buys the instrument, paying between $400 and $500. If he moves away, he tries to sell it, but if unable to do so, he must go off and leave it. In 1968 a Japanese transistor-radio company started putting in a transistor telephone system in La Paz. When ready, it will probably cut the price of instruments by more than half and allow thousands of people to get phones.

While not as bad off as Bolivia, Peru and Ecuador also need thousands of new telephone circuits. And all three countries need improved

Family industries are common in the countries of the central Andes. In Bolivia near Lake Titicaca a man, his wife, and his children produce rattles for fiestas

mail services. Generally, there are few if any carriers to make regular mail deliveries. Any carrier service that exists is slow, requiring a week to deliver a letter that would arrive in a day or two in Europe or the United States. People and businesses expecting mail rent post office boxes, or *apartados*. A letter sent special delivery to a man's home address may eventually be carried to him by a special carrier if regular carriers do not exist, as in Bolivia. Or it may just be held at the general delivery window. Many people register even letters that contain nothing of value, for clerks tamper with registered mail less frequently than with ordinary letters.

Light Industries

The second panel on doors of the Economics Building of Quito's Central University shows a large cogwheel and a smoking factory, symbolizing industry. The early Spaniards turned some of the Indian handcrafts into industries. For instance, the Spaniards promoted the making of garments for commercial purposes. The officials, adventurers, and homeseekers coming from Europe provided a market for these goods, which the Indians produced in their homes. In time the increase in local families and immigration created enough of a market for home industries to give way to factories. This was particularly true for clothes, and still today in all three countries of the central Andes the production of textiles is a major industry.

The Spaniards encouraged the Indians who did beautiful basketry to weave baskets for sale. They also encouraged the natives in the making of useful pottery, and Indians of today continue to weave baskets and to mold jars of clay. In all three countries Indians have long woven straw hats. Those made by the Otavalo Indians of Ecuador have proven particularly marketable and have been shipped to Colombia and Panama to be sold. They came to be called Panama hats by goldseekers in the nineteenth century who took the route across Panama on their way to California. In the twentieth century Panama hats grew so popular that they accounted for a fourth of Ecuador's exports. Gradually, lightweight hats of other materials took away the market until today Panama hats bring only a little export revenue into Ecua-

Using wood too small for sawing into lumber, a man gets ready to produce charcoal, one of the many small industries of Guayaquil, Ecuador. He stacks the wood around a pyramid of dirt, which keeps air from circulating well through the pile, and sets fire to the wood to char it

dor's treasury. Some factories for making the hats have had to close, and here is one industry that has in a measure returned to the home. Otavalo Indians say the finest hats are produced in the damp hours before dawn.

No remarkably large factories exist in the central Andes. Here and there small ones produce soap, candles, foodstuffs, tobacco products, wine, rubber products, medicines, toilet articles, furniture, sandals, and cement. Many of these establishments survive only because the workers receive low pay and put in long hours. Although governments set minimum wages and length of working days, a factory hiring a small number of laborers often avoids notice even though it fails to meet certain standards. Many labor unions exist—so many, in fact, they remain small and often fail to achieve their ends. Each one frequently goes its separate way, perhaps controlled by a man or family whose interests are mainly personal. The workers hardly benefit, and they won't as long as the leaders look down on them, which is often the case. One of the most effective weapons of any union is the strike, but when a man can barely remain alive on his income, he hardly dares cut off that income

196

for even a few days. As a result, strikes usually end before much has been accomplished. A slightly brighter picture can be found in the mining industries of Bolivia and Peru.

Heavy Industries

About the only heavy industries in the central Andes are mining, petroleum production, and the making of steel. More than half of Bolivia's revenue comes from mining, and Peru also depends heavily on its minerals. The labor forces in the mines amount to thousands of men, so relatively powerful unions can be formed. Because the governments lose export duties if the mines do not operate, officials keep a much closer eye on activities in the mines than they do on small-scale

A winery on the Guayas River helps to make Guayaquil the leading industrial center of Ecuador

A small train loaded with tin ore emerges from one of the mines in the "rich hill" of Potosí. At least three hundred mines have been dug into the mountain

factories. As a result, the well-to-do men who own or manage the mines have to pay attention to laws pertaining to wages and hours in order to prevent strikes. Tin rates first among Bolivian minerals, and lead, silver, copper, antimony, and wolfram are also found. Peru produces copper, lead, zinc, and several other minerals in salable quantities. Silver, gold, lead, copper, and sulfur have been mined in Ecuador but always on a small scale.

Of growing importance is the production of petroleum. Outside firms, many from the United States, have developed the oil fields since none of the local people knew how to do so. Profitable wells have been drilled in both Peru and Bolivia, but Ecuadorian production has not been great. In 1968 and 1969 oil caused a rift between Peru and the United States. In August, 1968, President Belaúnde's government reached an agreement with International Petroleum Corporation (IPC), a Canadian subsidiary of Standard Oil of New Jersey, by which IPC gave up its claims to the La Brea y Pariñas oil field in Peru's northwest. In exchange the Peruvian government dropped its demands that IPC pay an extra $144,000,000 in taxes (IPC was already Peru's biggest taxpayer). IPC received the right to continue prospecting and refining

198

in the area. Many Peruvians, rightists as well as leftists, accused Belaúnde of "selling out." They felt IPC had entered the La Brea y Pariñas area illegally and should not only quit the oil fields there but pay the taxes as well.

A military junta, using the petroleum controversy as its immediate excuse, ousted Belaúnde in October and seized the government. General Juan Velasco Alvarado took charge, declared the agreement with IPC illegal, and sent armed forces to the northwest to confiscate IPC holdings there. The United States government promptly announced it would review its Peruvian loan program. However, it refrained from immediate drastic action and by January, 1969, had recognized the junta government. When this did not relieve the situation, the United States threatened to cut off aid to Peru but in April found a loophole that allowed it to postpone taking such a step. Other foreign petroleum and

Aiding the Bolivian economy as it flows, petroleum is carried through pipelines that stretch across the southeastern part of the country near the border of Argentina

mineral holdings in Peru were not troubled at the time. When the new government invited more foreign investment in Peru, it received a flood of applications. Industrialists in Peru hope to build a steel industry and already have a small one underway. Since Peru has coal fields, steel mills may prove profitable, but Ecuador and Bolivia either lack coal or have not exploited their fields sufficiently to develop industries that require large amounts of the fuel.

Trouble Areas

Particularly in Bolivia and Ecuador the people complain that American firms exploit them industrially. They ignore the fact that other foreign companies have holdings in their lands and that many industries would not exist without foreign backing or management. Even though Bolivia had to call back many of the foreigners it tried to get rid of after the revolution of 1952, complaints continue to be made. Students, of course, decry the control of any industry by an outside capitalist country. At the same time, American and other foreign investors in the central Andes wail that they are being exploited by the governments there. They decry new taxes and export duties and wish they could return to the days when it was really possible to make huge profits abroad. The fact that they remain, however, indicates they must get reasonable returns on their investments.

The emphasis put on family unity causes trouble in industries in Bolivia, Ecuador, and Peru. Whenever a man starts any sort of enterprise, he is expected to hire his relatives for all but the menial jobs. As a consequence, his most important helpers may be his most useless ones. If he could freely hire capable men, his business would have a better chance of succeeding and growing. But even if he realizes this, he loyally gives out jobs to cousins, uncles, and in-laws. (The same family loyalty carries into politics, and any man who gets into office is expected to help all his relatives acquire political jobs.) Also a source of difficulty, central Andes businessmen seldom allow finances for maintenance of plants and equipment. A factory may fall apart while supposedly showing a profit because no one took into account upkeep and repairs.

A section of the busy harbor at Callao, Peru's major seaport and a base for fishing vessels

Fish

The middle panel on the Economics Building door shows a fishing boat, a net, and some fish. Great schools of valuable fish exist off the coasts of Peru and Ecuador, and Peru actively engages in capturing them. They do not go to feed the starving masses, but are primarily for sale abroad. Large quantities of fish are ground into meal, one of Peru's major exports. Why an equally profitable fish-meal industry has failed to develop in Ecuador puzzles outside observers.

Foreign fishing boats find themselves in trouble if they come too close to Peruvian and Ecuadorian shores. Both countries claim that their waters extend two hundred miles from their coasts. Many foreign nations, including the United States, refuse to recognize territorial rights beyond twelve miles. In the late 1960s some American fishing vessels have been held by Ecuador or Peru. Some of them have had to pay fines of more than $10,000 apiece to get released and have lost several days of fishing time besides. The United States Senate has passed a measure to reimburse companies whose boats are treated thus and to take the money out of aid funds earmarked for Peru and Ecuador. Naturally, this brings screams of protest from these nations of the central Andes, and it appears likely that the Organization of American States will have to try to work out rules concerning fishing rights.

Agriculture

Below the portrayal of fishing on the doors of the Economics Building are two agricultural panels, one showing the raising of crops and the other concerned with livestock. Throughout the central Andes agriculture is highly important, and in Ecuador it ranks as the number one industry. Important crops include corn, wheat, barley, beans, potatoes, grapes, oranges, lemons, apples, and cacao. Peru grows acres of good-quality cotton, while Ecuador produces a cotton of poorer quality. Both Ecuador and Peru raise large quantities of rice. Coca fulfills local needs for narcotic leaves and is exported to make cocaine. Sugarcane covers many acres, especially in Peru and Ecuador, and sugar refining constitutes an important industry. Ecuador's sugar goes to answer local uses, but Peru exports some. Coffee grows in the highlands of all three countries.

The main money-making crop of the central Andes is bananas, primarily grown in Ecuador though Peru produces some. This fruit brings Ecuador more revenue than any other single product, and most banana plantations are locally controlled. While Central Americans can object that their banana industry rests in foreign hands, Ecuadorians cannot. Although many agricultural workers rely on age-old practices, modernization has reached the banana industry. Helicopters spray large planta-

New types of corn have been introduced in Bolivia to increase the yield per acre. This is Cuban yellow corn, which gives double the yield, and is faster-growing and more nutritious than native corn

202

tions to keep pests under control, and plastic bags serve to protect heads of bananas while they're being shipped. Even so, large numbers of Negroes, mulattoes, mestizos, and Indians perform tedious hand labor to raise, harvest, and ship bananas. They receive poor wages, yet they fare well compared to people in the highlands. The average income along the coast, about $200 a year, is twice as high as that in the mountains.

Altiplano Farming

In the Andes many Indians farm much as their ancestors did. A man may still use a foot plow—a pointed board that the farmer shoves into the ground by stepping down on a crossbar. In some cases people seem to have forgotten what their ancestors knew. As you drive through the country, you can see any number of fields where the soil has been plowed up and down a hill instead of around it. In time, erosion ruins such fields. One of the great problems on the altiplano, of course, is controlling the supply of water. A river may flood the land between November and April, but dwindle away to a trickle during the dry season. Large areas have a year-round dry spell. Building dams for water control costs more than the governments care to spend. Besides, people in government come from the upper classes, and they are often indifferent to the needs of the Indians.

Agricultural technicians from Europe and North America and Peace Corps workers do more to educate the Indian farmers than most white people of the central Andes. Many Indians who raise sheep don't know how to shear them. They sell the sheep, often for a small profit after the animals are grown, and someone else reaps the good income from wool. They also sell livestock, both sheep and cattle, raised for butchering. The outsiders who want to assist the Indians teach them how to shear, butcher, cure hides, and accomplish other tasks they should know in order to gain more of the profits to be made in raising livestock. Men who raise llamas have had to learn to keep them back from good highways. Llamas seem to be unusually flighty and don't appear to understand the danger of cars as well as some animals do. Many of these

A Peace Corps agricultural extension worker in Bolivia's Cochabamba valley, George Wright talks to a group of farmers about a lame mule

Andean camels have been killed when they have run suddenly in front of vehicles. The animals have no difficulty when they graze along rougher roads, however, because trucks and cars cannot travel over these at high speeds.

A Brighter Tomorrow

Prophets continually foresee better days ahead for the countries of the central Andes. Perhaps these "fortune-tellers" think conditions can't get worse. Naturally, they can get worse, as Peruvians discovered in 1967. For years the sol, Peru's monetary unit, had held stable at about five cents in United States currency. The value started falling in 1967 and ended at about half its former level. Prices immediately went up, but not wages, and slum-dwellers and farmers of the altiplano wondered how they could survive. A third of Lima's one million people lived in shanty areas and saw no possible hope for improving their situation. Conditions are even worse in Bolivia and Ecuador. Estimates say that two-thirds of the 600,000 people in Guayaquil occupy slums. Perhaps half of the people in La Paz live in poverty, though their homes look better than those in poor sections of Lima and Guayaquil because they are of adobe instead of scrap lumber, metal, and cardboard. Quito has fewer poor people only because it lacks industries to attract men looking for jobs.

Action in Peru

It is not enough to say something should be done for the poor. Action must be taken. But the well-to-do people of the central Andes fear action that will improve conditions for people who have long been held down. They dread peaceful revolution as well as violent change and blindly ignore the fact that one or the other will probably come. So talk goes on while little gets done. However, in 1968 some Peruvian officials

Backward progress in Peru: A suburb of Trujillo, Peru, receives a sewage system long after the houses have been built. House construction proceeds faster than the laying of sewage-disposal facilities in much of South America

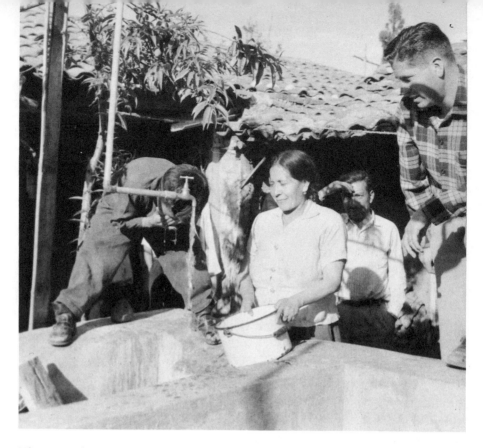

This Ecuadorian family enjoys the newly installed convenience of a potable water system

took steps to make drastic changes. President Belaúnde's finance minister called for increased income and business taxes and introduced taxes on property, a type of assessment that should reach the man who can afford to pay it. When the military junta took over the government in October, it made a persistent effort to enforce the new tax programs. Peruvian legislation called for more taxes to be withheld before salaries and dividends are paid. Some taxes in all three countries were already being withheld, usually from the income of the man who earned a fixed salary. The collection of taxes from nonsalaried men in the central Andes has long been something of a joke. In Bolivia, for instance, a businessman decides how much he wants to pay in taxes for a year. He hires an accountant to juggle the books until they show the businessman should pay the sum he has decided on. By similar dodges, people in Ecuador and Peru also evade their tax responsibilities. If Peru's new system helps correct this situation, the other countries will probably try to follow suit. Of course, it remains to be seen if the increased revenues will mean increased benefits for the poor, as Peru's government claims.

Smugglers' Paradise

If local products of the central Andes countries are to bring higher profits, efforts must be made to eliminate smuggling. Most good-quality shoes for sale in Bolivia come across the border from Brazil without a duty being paid. Plastic goods in all three countries frequently arrive illegally. Smugglers bring their articles to unwatched border areas by burro or small boat. Here they meet associates who live in the central Andes and turn the goods over to them. By whatever means they possess, the men receiving the products transport them to highways

Indians from the altiplano sometimes pack goods and themselves into the backs of trucks to go to market. At checkpoints like this one in Bolivia, they must unload everything if the inspectors decide to check for smuggled goods

and there load them into trucks. Of course, there are checkpoints set up, where trucks have to stop while officials paw through any goods being carried, but smugglers know of most such places. They ride to near the checkpoints, unload their "treasures," and go across country on foot or burro to escape being checked. At one hillside area in La Paz almost everything for sale has been smuggled in. Everybody, in government and out, knows this and pays no attention. Many new local industries could be launched if smuggling came to an end.

Once the Latin America Free Trade Association begins to operate, smuggling should become unprofitable because goods would be able to move freely among the countries of South America. Some people think the LAFTA will cure many ills as it creates a common-market area in the Southern Hemisphere. But at the rate it is being set up, LAFTA will not brighten the immediate future. Planned in 1960, it fails to appeal to

A practical education is provided at the social center at Coipasi in Bolivia, where farm women learn sewing, weaving, cooking, mending, washing and ironing. The center was built by the rural community and is also used as a meeting place and general social center

countries that fear surrendering any of their individual rights to the international controlling agencies necessary to make a common market work. Peru joined the association in the beginning, but Bolivia and Ecuador showed reluctance to belong. Early plans called for the LAFTA to be operating in the 1970s, but later estimates said the 1980s.

This above All

As has already been shown, the biggest advances needed in the central Andes are in education. Not just schoolbook knowledge is required. People must learn better agricultural practices and ways of improving living conditions. They must learn how to fill semiskilled jobs. They must understand the value of hygiene and sanitation. It is not enough to depend on the flocks of common black vultures and the huge, rare Andean condor (national bird of Ecuador) to handle garbage disposal. Warmth and energy for people on the altiplano need to come from sources other than coca leaves. People must develop respect for life and property. The upper classes need to lose their fear of the lower classes and allow them more advantages, while the groups within the lower classes must lose their distrust of one another. Until advances are shared on all levels by all groups, the nations as a whole will progress very slowly. No matter how bright the future looks to the prophets, education that results in definite changes will have to come before Peru, Bolivia, or Ecuador will be livable for all peoples, let alone a paradise.

Other Books to Enjoy

GENERAL

Latin America: A Cultural History, by Germán Arciniegas. New York: Alfred A. Knopf, 1967.

*The First Book of the Incas, by Barbara L. Beck. New York: Franklin Watts, 1966.

†*Andean Culture History,* by Wendell C. Bennett and Junius B. Bird. Garden City, N.Y.: Doubleday, 1964.

†*Spain in America, 1450-1581,* by Edward Gaylord Bourne. New York: Barnes & Noble, 1962.

**Hello South America,* by David Bowen. New York: W. W. Norton, 1964.

Conquistadores, Patricia de Fuentes, ed. New York: Grossman, 1963.

Fall of the Incas, by Shirley Glubok. New York: Macmillan, 1967.

†*Inside South America,* by John Gunther. New York: Harper & Row, 1967.

A History of Latin America from the Beginnings to the Present, rev. ed., by Hubert Herring. New York: Alfred A. Knopf, 1968.

Kon-Tiki and I, by Erik Hesselberg. Chicago: Rand McNally, 1950.

†*Kon-Tiki: Across the Pacific by Raft,* by Thor Heyerdahl. Chicago: Rand McNally, 1950.

The Andean Republics: Bolivia, Chile, Ecuador, Peru, by William Weber Johnson and the editors of *Life.* New York: Time, 1965.

Pre-Inca Art and Culture, by Hermann Leicht. New York: Orion, 1960.

Latin America: The Eleventh Hour, by Gary MacEoin. New York: Kenedy, 1962.

**The Story of the Incas,* by Robin McKown. New York: G. P. Putnam, 1966.

**Away to the Lands of the Andes,* by Albert J. Nevins. New York: Dodd, Mead, 1962.

**Indians of the Americas,* by Matthew W. Stirling and others. Washington, D.C.: National Geographic, 1966.

†*Latin America,* by Tad Szulc. New York: Atheneum, 1966.

The Latin American Tradition, by Charles Wagley. New York: Columbia University Press, 1968.

PERU

Daily Life in Peru under the Last Incas, by Louis Baudin. New York: Macmillan, 1962.

**Gold and Gods of Peru,* by Hans Baumann. New York: G. P. Putnam, 1963.

†*Lost City of the Incas,* by Hiram Bingham. New York: Atheneum, 1963.

†*Peru,* by G. H. S. Bushnell. New York: Frederick A. Praeger, 1963.

**Let's Visit Peru,* by John C. Caldwell. New York: John Day, 1962.

Peru and the United States 1900-1962, by James Charles Carey. Notre Dame, Ind.: University of Notre Dame Press, 1964.

Daily Life in Ancient Peru, by Hans Dietrich Disselhoff, trans. by Alisa Jaffa. New York: McGraw-Hill, 1967.
*Art of Ancient Peru, by Shirley Glubok. New York: Harper & Row, 1966.
*Pizarro and the Conquest of Peru, by Cecil Howard. New York: American Heritage, 1968.
Farewell to Eden, by Matthew Huxley and Cornell Capa. New York: Harper & Row, 1964.
Planning for Development in Peru, by Daniel R. Kilty. New York: Frederick A. Praeger, 1967.
The Forest Calls Back, by Jack Mendelsohn. Boston: Little, Brown, 1965.
†The Heights of Macchu Picchu, by Pablo Neruda, trans. by Nathaniel Tarn. New York: Farrar, Straus & Giroux, 1967.
*The Riddle of the Incas: The Story of Hiram Bingham and Machu Picchu, by James Norman. New York: Hawthorn, 1968.
Peru, by Ronald J. Owens. New York: Oxford University Press, 1963.
The Peru Traveler, by Selden Rodman. New York: Meredith, 1967.
Desert Kingdoms of Peru, by Victor W. Von Hagen. New York: New York Graphic Society, 1965.

BOLIVIA

†The Bolivian National Revolution, by Robert J. Alexander. Washington, D.C.: Savile Book, 1965.
*The First Book of Bolivia, by William E. Carter. New York: Franklin Watts, 1963.
Bolivia, A Land Divided, by Harold Osborne. New York: Oxford University Press, 1964.

ECUADOR

Ecuador: Constitutions and Caudillos, by George I. Blanksten. New York: Russell, 1964.
Mission to the Headhunters, by Frank and Marie Drown. New York: Harper & Row, 1961.
The Savage My Kinsman, by Elisabeth Elliot. New York: Harper & Row, 1961.
Four Years among the Ecuadorians, by Freidrich Hassurek. Carbondale, Ill.: Southern Illinois University Press, 1967.
Ecuador, Country of Contrasts, by Lilo Linke. London: Oxford University Press, 1960.
Class, Kinship and Power in an Ecuadorian Town, by Norman E. Whitten, Jr. Stanford, Calif.: Stanford University Press, 1965.

* *Written especially with young readers in mind*
† *Paperback edition available*

213

Historical Highlights

214

PERU

1820 José de San Martín starts liberation of Peru

1821 San Martín proclaims Peru's independence

1827 Simón Bolívar withdraws and José de La Mar becomes president

1865 Spain starts an unsuccessful attempt to regain her lost colonies

1872 Manuel Pardo introduces civilian rule

1875 Henry Meiggs begins the railway that bankrupts Peru

1879 Spain recognizes Peru's independence

1886 Andrés Cáceres introduces a period of peace

1895 Nicolas de Pierola leads a revolt and becomes president

1918 Augusto Leguia starts a dictatorship that ends in 1930

1923 Haya de la Torre founds the APRA party

1929 A treaty settles disputes from the War of the Pacific

1941 Peru takes land from Ecuador

1947 Thor Heyerdahl sails on the raft Kon-Tiki

1960 The Latin American Free Trade Association is planned, and Peru joins

1963 Fernando Belaúnde becomes president

1967 The sol is devalued

1968 Belaúnde is unseated and General Juan Velasco Alvarado takes over

BOLIVIA

1809 One of the earliest rebellions against Spain breaks out in Sucre

1825 José de Sucre secures Bolivia's independence

1828 President Sucre leaves

1836-39 Andrés Santa Cruz heads a federation of Peru and Bolivia

1841 José Ballivián defeats Peruvian invaders under Augustín Gamarra

1848 Manuel Belzu becomes president but fails to keep promises to Indians

1864 Mariano Melgarejo starts a reign of terror

1879-83 Bolivia and Peru fight Chile in the War of the Pacific

1900 La Paz becomes the unofficial capital

1904 Bolivia accepts a treaty concerning her lost seacoast

1932-35 Bolivia loses the Chaco War with Paraguay

1943 Gualberto Villarroel and the National Revolutionary Movement win control

1946 Villarroel is assassinated

1952 The country's most important revolution takes place

1962 Bolivia breaks diplomatic relations with Chile

1964 Paz Estenssoro and the MNR lose power

1966 René Barrientos takes power

1967 Cuban communists start guerrilla warfare, but Ernesto Che Guevara is shot

1969 Gen. Alfredo Ovando Candia overthrows government of Siles-Salinas

ECUADOR

1822 José de Sucre wins Ecuador's independence; San Martín and Bolívar meet in Guayaquil. Ecuador joined to Gran Colombia

1829 Sucre defeats La Mar of Peru

1830 Sucre is killed; Flores becomes dictator, separates Ecuador from Gran Colombia

1832 Ecuador claims the Galápagos Islands

1845 Flores is exiled and civil war breaks out

1860 Gabriel García ends civil war, becomes dictator

1875 García is murdered and twenty years of civil unrest start

1895 Eloy Alfaro is elected president but has to fight for a year to take office

1904 Land is lost to Brazil

1912 President Alfaro dies at the hands of a mob

1916 Land is lost to Colombia

1925-48 Period of great political instability; several presidents in succession

1940 Arroyo establishes a police state

1960 Velasco Ibarra takes office, is forced out again after political turmoil over economic problems

1963 Arosemena ousted; program of economic and social reforms begun

1967 Ecuador disputes over fishing rights with United States

1968 Velasco Ibarra starts his fifth term as president

215

Index

Furniture and utensils, 29, 30, 32, 36, 43, 44, 130, 135, 148-149, 170, 196

Galápagos Islands, 36-37, 107, 116
Gamarra, Augustín, 69-71, 88, 89
Garcia Moreno, Gabriel, 112, 113
González Prada, Manuel, 78-79
Gosseal, Pedro, 185
Government, 14, 21, 23, 39, 43, 48-49, 57, 59-62, 65-67, 69-72, 73-74, 75-76, 77-83, 85-91, 93-95, 97-101, 103, 105-110, 112-120, 144, 158-159, 168, 169, 178, 180, 182, 191, 196, 198-200, 204, 207-209, 210
Gran Colombia, 66-67, 69, 87, 105-107
Grau, Ricardo, 184
Guano, 36, 43, 49, 71-72
Guayaquil, Ecuador, 8, 13, 66-67, 106, 108, 110, 111, 113, 114, 115, 120, 138, 156, 191, 192, 196, 197, 207
Guayaquil, Gulf of, 19-20, 54
Guayasamín, Osvaldo, 185-186
Guevara, Ernesto "Che," 99-100
Guinea pigs, 23, 26, 43

Haciendas, 64, 80, 90, 95, 96-97, 105, 107, 113, 114-115, 132, 135, 191
Handcrafts, 10, 19-20, 21, 26, 29-30, 31, 128, 129, 130, 148, 172, 195-196
Haya de la Torre, Victor Raul, 78-79, 80-81
Headhunters, 34-35
Health, 48, 77, 80, 102, 106-107, 121, 153, 164, 165-168, 169, 171, 211
Hernandez, Daniel, 183-184
Heyerdahl, Thor, 50-51
Holidays and festivals, 42, 45, 134, 149-150, 172-174, 175, 187, 190, 194
Holzmann, Rudolfo, 176-177
Horses, 54, 55, 63
Hospitals, 165-166, 167-168
Housing, 10, 21, 23, 27, 29, 30, 36, 43, 47, 77, 81, 96, 133-135, 170, 206, 207
Huaca cultures, 21, 30
Huáscar, 48-49, 53-54, 56
Huayna Capac, Inca, 48-49, 53
Humboldt, (Peru) Current, 49-50
Hunting, 12, 21, 26, 30, 31, 33, 36

Icaza, Jorge, 179
Inca Indians, 11, 14-16, 18-19, 25, 30, 37-58, 87, 173, 177, 183, 189
Independence, 64-67, 72, 85, 86, 88-89, 105
Indians, 10-12, 14-16, 18-60, 62-63, 71, 72, 77, 78, 79, 80, 81, 83, 87, 88, 95-97, 98-99, 102, 105, 107, 110, 117, 119, 123-137, 141, 148, 151, 158, 165, 167, 168, 169-171, 173, 175, 177, 179, 183, 184, 185, 190, 195-196, 204, 207, 209, 210
Industries, 15, 40, 58, 61, 75, 76-77, 79, 82, 93, 94, 95-97, 100, 113, 115, 119, 121, 138, 155, 194, 195-202, 207, 210
Insects, 11, 21, 24, 31, 33, 43, 73, 167, 204
International relations, 70-71, 72, 73, 74-75, 80, 81-83, 88-89, 91, 93-94, 95, 99-101, 103, 106-108, 115-116, 119-120, 164, 178, 198-202, 209, 210-211
Iquitos, Peru, 32, 34, 36, 76, 142, 192
Irigoyen, Juan, 164, 165
Irrigation, 13, 22, 39, 80, 188
Islands, 19-20, 36-37, 40, 49, 50, 51
Iturriaga, Enrique, 177

Jivaro Indians, 34-35
Joffré, Sara, 178
Jungles, 11, 12, 13, 14, 15, 30-36, 48, 98, 115, 128, 133, 169

Kon-Tiki, 50-51

Labor, 45-46, 47-48, 56, 60, 62, 73, 76, 77, 80, 81, 94, 95, 96-97, 99, 102, 115, 123, 124, 126, 127, 129, 130, 131, 132, 133-137, 138, 143, 153, 163, 173, 189, 196-198, 200, 204, 207, 211
La Gasca, Pedro de, 60
Laja, Bolivia, 63
La Mar, José de, 69, 87, 106
Land formation, 17-18
Languages, 41-42, 157, 158, 180, 181
La Paz, Bolivia, 61, 66, 67, 84, 85, 91, 92, 93, 96, 100, 103, 122, 133, 139, 159, 164, 165, 177-178, 186, 189, 190, 192, 194, 207, 210
Laredo Unzueto, Jaime, 176
Latin America Free Trade Association, 210-211
Laws and justice, 26, 35, 44-45, 55-56, 57, 59, 60, 62, 79-80, 83, 136, 196, 198, 202, 208
Legends, 34, 39-42, 170-171, 185
Leguía, Augusto Bernardino, 80
Libraries, 142, 161, 179, 180
Lima, Peru, 50, 56, 57, 62, 64, 65-67, 69-70, 73, 75, 78, 79, 151, 157, 162, 173-174, 177-178, 181, 186, 192, 207
Literacy, 95, 96, 108
Literature, 37, 78, 108, 161, 178-181
Livestock, 23, 26, 29, 39, 43, 44, 45, 48, 54, 55, 56, 62, 63, 82, 123, 127, 170, 176, 193, 202, 204-205

219

222

About the Author

CHARLES PAUL MAY has traveled extensively in Latin America. He visited Peru, Bolivia, and Ecuador in 1967 and returned for a longer stay in 1968. In each country he visited inland cities and villages as well as the more easily accessible coastal ones. He talked with all manner of people, using the help of missionaries, teachers, and Peace Corps workers from the U.S. He reported, "I sat in on some little theater rehearsals and even served as a prop for one until the lamp post I was representing was repaired. At one restaurant in Ecuador the manager gave me my meal because I sat and talked with his two sons who were studying English in school and got little chance to practice on anyone outside their classes. It was an out-of-the-way place, since I generally avoid the very touristy places where I meet only other travelers."

Mr. May is a welcome speaker at libraries and book fairs where he illustrates his travelogue with his own color slides. He has written three World Neighbors and many other books for young people, and his photography has appeared in such publications as *National Geographic, Travel,* and the *New York Times.*

World Neighbors

Written to introduce the reader to his contemporaries in other lands and to sketch the background needed for an understanding of the world today, these books are well-documented, revealing presentations. Based on first-hand knowledge of the country and illustrated with unusual photographs, the text is informal and inviting. Geographical, historical, and cultural data are woven unobtrusively into accounts of daily life. Maps, working index, chronology, and bibliography are useful additions.

ALASKA Pioneer State, by Norma Spring
THE ARAB MIDDLE EAST, by Larry Henderson
ARGENTINA, PARAGUAY & URUGUAY, by Axel Hornos
AUSTRALIA & NEW ZEALAND, by Lyn Harrington
AUSTRIA & SWITZERLAND Alpine Countries, by Bernadine Bailey
BRAZIL Awakening Giant, by Kathleen Seegers
CANADA Young Giant of the North, by Adelaide Leitch
CENTRAL AMERICA Lands Seeking Unity, by Charles Paul May
CHILE Progress on Trial, by Charles Paul May
CHINA & THE CHINESE, by Lyn Harrington
EQUATORIAL AFRICA New World of Tomorrow, by Glenn Kittler
GERMANY A Divided Nation, by Alma & Edward Homze
GREECE & THE GREEKS, by Lyn Harrington
INDIA Land of Rivers, by L. Winifred Bryce
ISRAEL New People in an Old Land, by Lily Edelman
ITALY Modern Renaissance, by Arnold Dobrin
JAPAN Crossroads of East and West, by Ruth Kirk
THE LOW COUNTRIES Gateways to Europe, by Roland Wolseley
MEDITERRANEAN AFRICA Four Muslim Nations, by Glenn Kittler
MEXICO Land of Hidden Treasure, by Ellis Credle
PERU, BOLIVIA, ECUADOR The Indian Andes, by Charles Paul May
SCANDINAVIA The Challenge of Welfare, by Harvey Edwards
THE SOVIET UNION A View from Within, by Franklin Folsom
SPAIN & PORTUGAL Iberian Portrait, by Daniel Madden
THE UNITED KINGDOM A New Britain, by Marian Moore
VIETNAM and Countries of the Mekong, by Larry Henderson
THE WEST INDIES Islands in the Sun, by Wilfred Cartey
YUGOSLAVIA, ROMANIA, BULGARIA, by Lila Perl